OtherWise Christian 2

OtherWise Christian 2:
Stories of Resistance

Edited by Mx Chris Paige

OtherWise Engaged Publishing

To Rabbi Josh —
with love and appreciation.
Shalom.
        Liam

First edition March 2020
Cover by Chris Paige
Cover image courtesy of Canva.com

ISBN: 978-1-951124-14-4 (Paperback)
ISBN: 978-1-951124-19-9 (Large Print Paperback)
ISBN: 978-1-951124-15-1 (Hardback)
ISBN: 978-1-951124-17-5 (Kindle)
eISBN: 978-1-951124-16-8
Audio ISBN: 978-1-951124-18-2

Published by OtherWise Engaged Publishing
http://otherwiseengaged4u.wordpress.com

Visit http://www.otherwisechristian.com

CONTENTS

Foreword

The book you are reading is long overdue. I know, because I have waited sooooo long for it—decades, in fact. Please bear with me as I introduce myself, for context.

I spent most of my teens and twenties trying to reconcile my firm belief in God and my firm belief that I was really a woman inside, notwithstanding what my body and the rest of the world told me. It was a difficult journey, made more so by the lack of information about transgender issues available to the general public.

When I entered seminary at the Pacific School of Religion in 1992, I never expected to be writing about transgender issues. However, I soon learned that there were no transgender-positive articles in any reputable academic journals of theology. Not any. I know because I did an exhaustive literature search using every tool that the 1990's could provide.

It took a few years, but my article "Toward a Christian Ethical Response to Transsexual Persons" was published in the journal *Theology and Sexuality* in 1997. I tried to keep a neutral voice, so as to be academically appropriate, while still offering affirming interpretations.

I quickly followed up with two essays published in anthologies of queer theology, boldly trying to address biblical "clobber passages" used to attack transgender people and attempting to show some of the ways that gender nonconforming people are present in the scriptures.

Since those days, a few transgender spiritual leaders have written books about transgender-positive theology, liturgy, and their own personal spiritual journeys. The output has been just a trickle and only a fraction of what we all know is out there waiting to be shared.

Frankly, there has been little interest in the publishing world in exploring transgender people's spiritual experiences. We are still told that we are too small of a niche audience. Meanwhile, many religious people are openly hostile toward us. Still, others think that everything important on "the issue" has already been said!

I went on to be ordained in 1998 as a minister in the Universal Fellowship of Metropolitan Community Churches. Even though it is a transgender-affirming denomination and had several prominent clergy who transitioned after ordination, I was the first person to go through the ordination process as an openly transgender person. It was rough. I tried so hard not to be pigeonholed as "the transgender minister" that I actively avoided the work on transgender perspectives that I had begun in seminary. There are so many ways that our voices get silenced.

When I met Chris Paige, well over a decade ago, there was a real spark of excitement. We discussed how we could create a community of people to share more deeply about transgender spiritual experience. I joined the board of the Interfaith Working Group, which was home to the Transfaith project. One of our goals at the time was to create a safe space to share our stories—stories which are so often overlooked or ignored. We wanted to create a true multi-faith spiritual community for transgender and gender non-conforming people.

That was so much easier said than done. It takes a lot of work to create and moderate such a forum, and I certainly lacked the gifts to contribute much to that effort. Moreover, I became distracted with my secular career as a judge—first as an administrative law judge and later as an elected trial court judge.

However, Mx Chris never wavered from their commitment to this mission of giving our voices a place to be heard. More recently, they wrote *OtherWise Christian: A Guidebook for Transgender Liberation,* which is novel in its scope, covering 25 years of transgender-affirming theological developments. It is the book that I always told myself that I would write, someday. However, I didn't. I couldn't. I got stuck in the 1990's.

In the time since I did my work, the world has changed, and our spiritual institutions have not kept up. People like Mx Chris who do not fit within the binary gender structure that we inherited have remained largely invisible in both the academy and the church. As a personal aside, my former spouse now identifies as non-binary, but I am the same, old-fashioned, gender-conforming femme that I was decades ago. I used to be cutting edge, but now I am passe!

Otherwise Christian 2: Stories of Resistance is yet another ground-breaking contribution from Mx Chris Paige. It is a book that brings together many different voices in one anthology, each one talking about a different lived experience, each one resisting what society has told us we should be. It accomplishes in book form the best of what we were striving to create online—a gathering of disparate voices, diverse stories, rallying in support of one another. This is so important (and still much needed today) because even the wisest among us has only our own limited experience to draw from. Each one of us benefits from hearing someone else's story. This is one of the best ways for us to learn.

Indeed, I discovered that one of the most important things about sharing our experiences is that it inevitably demonstrates that spiritual communities are not as homogeneous as we have been led to believe. We are both homogenous *and* heterogeneous. We are alike in so many ways, but different in others—all of which are important. For too long, we have hidden our differences in shame. Yet, balancing an understanding of both our similarities and our differences is the key to creating a modern spirituality that can enrich us all.

I am deeply honored that Mx Chris invited me to contribute to this important work. I am sure that you will find it as enlightening, encouraging, mind-stretching, and challenging as I do.

Blessings and Peace,
Rev. Victoria S. Kolakowski (Retired)
Oakland, California

Preface

For just as the body is one
and has many members,
and all the members of the body,
though many, are one body,
so it is with Christ.

1 Corinthians 12:12 NRSV

In *OtherWise Christian: A Guidebook for Transgender Liberation*, I focused primarily on digging into scripture, from Genesis to Galatians. Yet, for Christians to understand and appreciate OtherWise-gendered people will require more than just an affirming understanding of the biblical text, it will require more than survey questionnaires and textbooks with terms and definitions. To really understand OtherWise-gendered folk will require experience in authentic relationship with diverse OtherWise-gendered people who are making our way in the world.

Too often, when an (openly) transgender person walks through the door of a church, they become a *de facto* one-person transgender education task force. This can be problematic for both the individual and the congregation. First and foremost, the individual may have come bearing burdens, not seeking to teach! Meanwhile, if you have met one person of transgender experience, you have met only one person of transgender experience. You are likely to learn about that one person's bias and experience, but you may miss out on the gender-full testimonies that would come from more diverse perspectives.

Meanwhile, the challenges facing people with intersex variations are similar, yet compounded by additional layers of stigma, shame, invisibility, and misinformation. I have long believed that endosex (that is, not intersex) transgender folk need to do a better job of working in solidarity with our intersex siblings. I am proud and grateful that five openly intersex people are included in this volume speaking from their own experience. Yet, we can (and will) do more. In fact, plans are already in motion (see Appendix A).

OtherWise Christian 2: Stories of Resistance endeavors to introduce you, briefly, to a range of OtherWise-gendered people. Drawing on relationships from my time with *The Other Side* magazine and with Transfaith, I reached out to friends and colleagues. I asked them to write about their lived experience and to connect that experience to scripture. There were a few cases where I asked for something more specific based on pre-existing sermons, publications, or personal sharing, but generally not. I read in awe as each story emerged, unique in its focus but with deep connections among them.

There is something profoundly intimate about editing someone's spiritual reflection. I have found editing this anthology to be truly sacred work. It has been an honor and a privilege in every sense of those words to shepherd this project. I do not take it for granted that this many folk, both brilliant and bruised, have trusted me with their words, despite differences in race, gender, sexuality, class, and religious perspective. Some are long-time friends, some are newer colleagues, and some are relationships that emerged directly out of this project.

Being actively in touch with about a dozen of these authors at any given time was also sobering. What you will not see generally reflected in this text are the details of hospitalizations and funerals, job losses and financial strains, mental health challenges and medication changes, school deadlines and family obligations, cross-country moves and international travel that occurred even just in the months that I was working to compile these reflections. Please understand that every one of these people is navigating serious real-life challenges, while making themselves vulnerable, not just to me, but to all of us through these chapters.

There are a million very good reasons why any one of them might have chosen not to take this risk with me or with us. There are a million more things that could have gone wrong as we worked through such sensitive topics and representations. Indeed, several authors dropped out because they could not make the time in their schedule for various reasons. So, I specifically want to honor and acknowledge the strength and courage of these authors. Their trust and commitment are the foundation upon which this anthology has grown.

I will continue blogging at **otherwisechristian.com** with news and links about other projects these authors are involved in, from churches to non-profits to consulting, from podcasts to blogs to other books. I hope you will join in their efforts, as well as considering the variety of other books from OtherWise Engaged Publishing.

Mx Chris Paige
March 2020

Introduction

O taste and see that the LORD is good;
happy are those who take refuge in [God].

Psalm 34:8 NRSV

Transgender men, transgender women, and non-binary people all have our own particular sets of challenges and risk factors as we navigate the world. In a Western worldview, these are three major categories of transgender experience. Meanwhile, people with intersex variations may or may not be transgender, may or may not be identified with the binary (male or female), may or may not use "intersex" as an identity. OtherWise-gendered people may be "straight," same-gender-loving, asexual, bisexual/pansexual, or have some other way to name their interests. Some may be open and public about their gender history, while others may be nondisclosing or low-disclosure. This is just a small sample of some of the kinds of diversity that you may encounter among OtherWise-gendered people in the Western world, before we even touch on language and culture.

This diversity of new vocabulary can be confusing and overwhelming to some as new shared understandings are being fashioned. Most of us have been raised in a culture that claimed that there are "two and only two, mutually exclusive genders, defined strictly and easily, based on biology at birth" (see Appendix A of this volume, as well as *OtherWise Christian*, chapter 2). For OtherWise-gendered folk, resisting that reductive gender ideology is not an intellectual question but, rather, a way of life in which we struggle to make our way through a world that tells us in so many ways that it would rather not be bothered with us at all. As you seek to understand our varied struggles, the language we use, and the way we conceptualize resistance, it is important to shift—away from simply trying to label and define us toward hearing our stories as testimonies of strength and resilience.

Imagine if you had been taught that "vanilla" and "chocolate" are the only kinds of ice cream that are possible. Would you be worried to learn about butter pecan and strawberry ice cream? Would you feel ill-prepared for Neapolitan, rocky road, or cotton-candy-flavored ice cream? How might you react to a soft serve cone dipped in chocolate, ice cream sandwiches, frozen yogurt, or gluten-free and nondairy vegan "ice cream"? With or without nuts? Whipped cream? And a cherry on top?

The variations are endless, but this complexity need not be threatening. You do not have to be an expert on every ingredient or every kind of ice cream just to enjoy a midnight snack or to take a grandchild out for a treat. In fact, questions to determine if your favorite confection qualifies properly as "chocolate" or "vanilla" are probably not so welcome when you are eager to have a taste.

Similarly, I invite you to give up on trying to put people into categories. Instead, I hope that you will try to enjoy the testimonies of the authors in this volume—as if they were the first sweet treat that you have had in years. Please don't waste your time worrying. Savor the flavors. Notice the sensations. Enjoy!

In the opening chapters of *OtherWise Christian 2*, you will find testimonies of trans feminine, trans masculine, non-binary, and intersex encounters with the Holy, as well as their encounters with patriarchy, embodiment, and liberation. Several of these reflections date as far back as 2001 and are some of the earliest published stories from transgender Christians (during what I call the "transgender spring"), though they have all been revised at least somewhat for re-publication here. These first offerings are intended to provide a very basic introduction to "vanilla." You will have an opportunity to get a taste, but please know that there are many other delicious flavors to come!

In the remainder of this book, you will find yet more stories of resistance. We will not tarry with "transgender 101" definitions. There are plenty of other books, blogs, and webinars for that. You can go elsewhere to sort through arguments about whether OtherWise-gendered people actually exist. If you are worried about whether we should be treated as inherently sick or sinful, you might not be ready to hear the wisdom that we have to share. Yet, we are here, living our best lives. Truly, truly, I tell you, we speak of what we know, and we testify to what we have seen (John 3:11a).

There are a wide range of (auto)biographical and anecdotal stories about transgender and intersex people to be found in the world already. This volume is different insofar as it assembles offerings that will make explicit connections between lived OtherWise experience and Christian tradition—and sometimes other traditions as well. Authors have been invited to offer a theological perspective grounded in their own magnificent lives. I have to warn you that we are boundary-busting folk who do not much like being confined in orderly boxes. But, we offer our testimonies just the same, drawing on our own histories, our own struggles, and our own relationships with the Divine. Let those accept it who can (Matthew 19:12b).

In a historic roundtable in the *Journal of Feminist Studies in Religion* (Spring 2018), Dr. Max Strassfeld, asks this question: "In what ways might we expand our analyses of prayer and ritual if we took the lives and resiliencies of trans women of color as religion?" (page 51). Strassfeld's question was offered in an academic context, but, in this volume, I invite you to open yourself in that way. Indeed, what if we look to OtherWise-gendered people to teach us about practices that nurture survival and sustainability? What if we trust OtherWise-gendered people to tell us something about what is most sacred? What might we learn about what makes life worth living?

Instead of working to stuff transgender experience into pre-existing categories of religious or Christian experience, I invite you to open your heart to listen to what OtherWise-gendered folk might have to teach you about the Divine, about holy laughter, about our most intimate relationships, and about fighting back against the principalities and powers of this world that bring death and despair. Listen for the rhythms that resonate between authors. Attend to both the themes that connect with your own life experiences, as well as those that differ. There are suggested scriptures and reflection questions at the end of each offering to assist you in processing and integrating what you have read.

Of course, no one collection can ever be definitive. There will always be yet more stories to be shared from God's gender-full goodness among us. Indeed, I am aware of some important gaps in this effort. Yet, I hope that this volume will give you a taste that will help you better to appreciate what is possible among God's people. I am grateful for the diverse array of folk who have trusted me enough to edit and publish their insights here. I pray that you will be blessed by their testimonies just as I have been.

Please check out **otherwisechristian.com** where you will find additional content related to the OtherWise Christian series, including news about other projects by these authors, more resources, as well as opportunities for further conversation.

Mx Chris Paige

Abbreviations

ESV English Standard Version

KJV King James Version

NASB New American Standard Bible

NIV New International Version

NLT New Living Translation

NKJV New King James Version

NRSV New Revised Standard Version

Section 1

Claiming Our Voices

Gender Diversity
and Christian Community

By Virginia Mollenkott

Like the cosmos itself,
God is about only two things:
diversity and communion.
The whole creation cannot be lying.

Richard Rohr

I believe the time has come for Christians to widen their welcome
to include the full range of human diversity, including gender diversity. I
believe this both because of the biological and psychological realities
around us and because of the message of gradually expanding inclusiveness
I see in scripture. I hope for a time when Christian congregations
everywhere will embrace all of God's creation as good.

Our society is currently ruled by a binary gender construct: a largely
unquestioned set of assumptions that there are only two sexes (male and
female) and that those born "male" are naturally drawn to what our society
happens to call "masculine" (including attraction to women only) and that
those born female are naturally drawn to what our society calls "feminine"
(including attraction to men only). It is a system that allows for only one set
of choices: Either a person must self-define as exclusively male or female,
or else admit to being unnatural, mutant, or abnormal.

Once a person has self-identified as female, social attitudes
conspire to blur any distinction between her biological sex and socially
assigned female gender roles, which for women tend to be either unpaid in
the private sphere or severely limited in the public sphere. If she refuses to
conform to the limitations of femininity, she will be labeled as
"controlling," "strident," or "lesbian." Many women are frightened into
conformity by such labels. Boys and men are also pressured into gender-
conformity through name calling, but in their case, the name-calling (such
as, "sissy," "weakling," "queen") teaches contempt for the feminine as that
which is weak, dependent, or passive.

Thus, gender control of females is achieved by extolling

3

"masculine" virtues but placing them beyond the reach of "real women," while gender control of men is achieved by degrading "femininity" so that no "real man" would ever want to be associated with it.

In the 20th century, both the women's movement and the movement for gay, lesbian, and bisexual civil rights have raised gender issues in very new and different ways. One of the most helpful contributions they have offered is the distinction among sexual orientation, gender identity, gender roles, and gender expression. Many of our discussions around gender confuse these four elements. Sexual orientation concerns the gender to which one is attracted. Gender identity refers to a person's "core" feeling of maleness, femaleness, or other. Gender role refers to a socially constructed correlation between one's biology and one's skills, attitudes, interests, and behavior. It is worth noting that these gender role expectations differ widely from culture to culture and from era to era. Gender expression refers to the way people present themselves through their clothing, body language, and behaviors, whether as masculine, feminine, or other.

Using this helpful lens, when we look at the realities of the creation around us, we discover a diversity for which we are not always prepared. Whether gay or "straight," many men are not drawn to masculine behaviors, attitudes, and roles, and many women are not drawn to feminine behaviors, attitudes, and roles. We see in all of creation, animal as well as human, both cross-sex and same-sex relationships. We see different cultures that have entirely divergent expectations of male roles and female roles.

We also find individuals who cannot authentically identify as male or female. Some people have chromosomes or partially developed sex organs that do not match their apparent gender. As many as four percent of all children are born with degrees of both male and female genitalia, and one person in five hundred has a chromosomal composition other than XX or XY. The presence of these intersex persons among us dispels the notion that the human race is built upon a clear-cut male-female polarity. People who self-identify as transgender also reflect in their testimony and experience the pain and struggle of trying to fit into a social construct that does not work.

In *Gender Trouble: Feminism and the Subversion of Identity*, Judith Butler pointed out that transgender people force us to confront the inadequacies of the male-female paradigm. They are "the exception, the strange, that give us the clue to how the mundane and taken-for-granted world of sexual meanings is constructed." By refusing (or being unable) to perform society's expected gender roles and presentations, by falling outside of the "normal" male-female polarity, transgender people reveal that the "taken for granted world of sexual categorization is a constructed one, indeed one that might well be constructed differently."

All of us are therefore called to confront the binary gender construct for our own good and the good of those who are transgender. Because gender roles are by no means equitable, binary gender assumptions and roles are devastating to all of us—"masculine men," "feminine women," and those somewhere in the middle.

Enormous numbers of heterosexual people are transgender in the sense that they transgress the gender-role assignments of our society's binary gender construct. There are many boys and men who do not like sports, machinery, or business, preferring poetry, knitting, or peace-making. Similarly, many girls and women have little tolerance for the roles our society defines as "feminine," preferring stock-market trades to childcare, or white-water rafting to a beautification day at the spa. Should people be forced to adjust their clothes, grooming, and behavior in order to fit a social abstraction? Or, is the huge amount of role transgression an indication that our male-female polarity has outlived its usefulness?

For several decades, transgender diversities have become increasingly obvious in various subcultures all over the planet. Meanwhile, most Christian churches have buried their heads in the sand of endless dialogue about whether or not it is compatible with Christian witness to ordain or provide union ceremonies for those members who happen to be gay or lesbian. While the church was looking the other way, gender issues became much more complex, and, as a consequence, much of the debate within church walls is increasingly irrelevant to the realities with which individuals are struggling.

For instance, now that some Christians are getting used to the idea of gayness and lesbianism as identities rather than choices, many people are realizing that such essentialism is only another limiting abstraction. Not that we choose our sexual orientation or gender presentation like flavors of ice cream. No. We choose them as the only way to live authentically. But, understanding how our society constructs "normalcy" can give us the freedom to move beyond static identifications—if a person needs such freedom to live authentically.

Does this leave us in total confusion? It certainly is an upheaval—but do we want to deal with reality, or delude ourselves by returning to a mythic time when men were primary and dominant, women were secondary and submissive, everybody was heterosexual, and folks were expected to repress or keep hidden any impulses to the contrary?

Jesus said, "I came that they may have life, and have it abundantly" (John 10:10b NRSV). That does not sound as though we are intended to shrink ourselves to fit into what our society happens to define as proper gender identities, roles, and presentations. In fact, as I read the Scriptures, I see a movement toward inclusion, toward a widening of the welcome to embrace all kinds of diversity, including gender diversity.

The creation story begins by affirming that God is neither male nor female, but both (Genesis 1:27). The first chapter of Genesis emphasizes that both male and female are made in the image of the Creator God. Both are equally created in the divine image of one Supreme Being—who therefore must be understood to encompass both maleness and femaleness and everything in between. According to scholars of Genesis, the original creature was the *adam*, an earth creature who was both male and female. It was only in response to the *adam*'s need for companionship that God put the *adam* into a deep sleep to divide the creature into what we now understand as male and female.

Regarding gender inclusion in scripture, perhaps the best example is that of the eunuch, a term that refers to castrated men or to people who are unable to have children. By modern understanding, the term includes intersex people and post-operative transsexuals and symbolically includes homosexuals and celibates. In ancient Israel, eunuchs were excluded from the Temple—and thus from the assembly of God's people (Deuteronomy 23:1), but the prophet Isaiah reverses that legislation, proclaiming inclusion and offering to faithful eunuchs "a monument and a name better than sons and daughters" (Isaiah 56:4–5 NRSV).

Jesus also spoke well of eunuchs in his discourse on marriage and divorce, classifying eunuchs as either "so from birth," or "made eunuchs by others," or those who "made themselves eunuchs for the sake of the kingdom of heaven" (Matthew 19:12 NRSV). This movement toward acceptance is capped by Acts 8:26–40, where a eunuch from Ethiopia is baptized into the new covenant community of Jews who are disciples of Jesus. This eunuch, symbolizing the community of ostracized sexual minorities, is among the first of the outcasts from ancient Israel to be welcomed into Jesus' discipleship of equals.

Jesus, whom Paul refers to as the Second Adam (1 Corinthians 15:45–47) also defied gender norms. He did not marry, although he had the religious obligation to do so at eighteen. He performed acts such as cooking or washing the feet of his disciples—acts culturally assigned to wives or slaves, not to a free male, and certainly not to a rabbi.

Contemporary Christians need to embody this same daring biblical inclusiveness toward all people of faith. This would entail simply accepting people's gender presentation at face value, approaching everyone as the human equals they are, and relaxing about gender—our own and everyone else's.

I dream of the day when Christian congregations will embrace the prophetic universalism of Isaiah: "For my house shall be called a house of prayer for all peoples. Thus say the Lord God, who gathers the outcasts of Israel: I will gather others to them besides those already gathered" (Isaiah 56:7–8 NRSV).

Franciscan ethicist and author Richard Rohr commented: "Like the cosmos itself, God is about only two things: diversity and communion. The whole creation cannot be lying." When Christian love is universal, then and only then will Christianity begin to be about those same things. Indeed, if Christianity is to survive as a living religion, such communion with diversity will have to come about. The whole of God's creation cannot be lying.

Notes

Dr. Virginia Mollenkott is the author of thirteen books and dozens of articles on feminist and liberating interpretations of scripture. She retired from college teaching in 1997, is grandmother to three teenagers, and is willing mentor to younger feminist scholars.

Please see Appendix B for additional information on counting people with intersex variations.

Judith Butler's *Gender Trouble: Feminism and the Subversion of Identity* was originally published in 1990 by Routledge and has since been republished numerous times.

This article was originally published in *The Other Side* magazine, Volume 37, Number 3 (May–June 2001). It was updated for this anthology.

Suggested scripture

Genesis 1:27—Made in the Image of God (see Chapter 6 of *OtherWise Christian*)

Isaiah 56:1–8—Reversal about eunuchs (and foreigners) in Isaiah (see Chapter 13 of *OtherWise Christian*)

Acts 8:26–40—Ethiopian Eunuch Traveler (see Chapter 15 of *OtherWise Christian*)

For further reflection

How have you been impacted by gender roles and expectations throughout your life?

Does having more than two gender options to consider cause confusion for you?

Mollenkott (following Rohr) suggests that God is all about diversity and communion. How is that similar or different to the assumptions that you may have learned in the church or other religious upbringing?

8

Body and Soul United

By Erin Swenson

*Just then his disciples returned
and were surprised to find him
talking with a woman.
But no one asked,
"What do you want?" or
"Why are you talking with her?"*

John 4:27 NIV

Today, while many denominations and faith groups continue to struggle over issues of sexuality and faith, few have really even scratched the surface of the many questions surrounding gender identity. Yet, questions around our notions of gender have the potential to be even more difficult than issues of sexuality, because the debate around gender identity is much less about how we behave and far more about who we are.

Gender identity is distinct from—and more basic than—sexual orientation. One's sense of being male or female precedes one's affections and attractions. Who we are is more basic than what we do or who we love. It is, therefore, in many ways a more explosive and dangerous issue for churches and communities that value homogeneity.

Years ago, I faced the ordeal of having to defend my own ordination as a Presbyterian minister. This challenge came because I decided, after twenty-three years of ordained ministry as a man, to change my gender. After sixteen months of contentious discussion and debate, in October 1996, the Presbytery of Greater Atlanta voted to sustain my ordination, making me the first mainline Protestant minister to undergo a gender transition and retain ordination.

All my life, I had pursued what appeared to be a normal life pattern in the desperate hope that no one would see the terrible truth about me— that I wanted to be female. This desire seemed against all reason and against all that seemed right and good to me. I could not explain these feelings, but I knew they were from the very core of my being. I prayed for deliverance from these strange longings, but none came.

As a young person, I was heavily involved in the church and was elected to my presbytery youth council, where I was encouraged to pursue the professional ministry. I was a member of my high school wrestling team and participated in many traditionally male hobbies such as carpentry and electronics. Yet, I could not shake this sense that the reality of who I knew myself to be was inconsistent with the male body into which I was born.

I spent enormous resources in trying to become the man that the church and society wanted me to be. I married at a relatively young age, hoping in vain that this would finally "answer" some need in me and free me from my gender burden. I not only entered psychotherapy, but also became a therapist myself, trying to understand and deal with my situation.

I struggled with depression, burying myself in work and responsibility in order to hide from the terrible truth within. I applied myself most diligently to the task of living and working as a male, and succeeded for many years. I even convinced myself that I could hold the truth within me for a lifetime—that I would die with my secret still intact.

However, the depression and denial took their toll on my health. Eventually, I lost my marriage, not because of my "gender problem," but because of my willingness to deny the truth and thereby destroy my self-respect and the respect of my partner. Finally, I decided I could sustain the lie no longer.

Ironically, in the years since I decided, at great personal cost, to end my deceitful life and devote myself to living a life that feels more authentic and truthful to myself and before God, I have often been accused of deceit. I have been told that my actions are a denial of both scripture's clear teaching and the goodness of my own creation, that I am lying to myself and to God, that I am bringing shame on the church, and confusing other Christians who might be struggling with their own sexual identity.

These charges are often infused with an anger that I have found difficult to understand. I have wondered why my decision seemed to spark such violent opposition. Many times, I felt like I had to defend myself from the existential rage of my accusers, more than from any real theological argument. It is as if the reality of who I am, a reality that clothes my own soul, threatens the very foundation of what they believe.

As I have wrestled with these questions, I have come to recognize that this anger is not only the anger of my accusers or the anger of my church. For a long time, this was my anger as well. I spent the best years of my life wringing just enough energy from myself to carry on as a husband, father, and minister against a personal reality that seemed wholly unacceptable not only to others, but to myself and God as well. It seemed that I had been excluded from the realm of heaven, that God was playing some kind of cosmic trick on me.

For much of my life, I thought I was alone in these struggles. Yet, over the years, I learned that many others experience the same intense conflict between traditional gender expectations and their own sense of who they are. Those whose gender identity does not match our identity as assigned at birth are referred to as "transgender."

I am not so arrogant as to believe that God somehow made me transgender to "teach the church a lesson." However, I do believe that God uses our lives to work out God's purposes. I believe the church's struggle with me—and with others who are transgender—parallels the church's struggle with itself. In a sense, the church has also been struggling with a gender change. The realities of transgender people force the church to confront this, whether it wants to or not.

Reconsidering the early Hebrew understanding of sexuality has helped shed light on this for me. In the ancient world, the male sex organs were viewed as sacred in ways that transcended all other aspects of human biology. In the sex act, the male was believed to deposit a complete microscopic human being into the woman's womb for safekeeping while it grew, nourished by the mother, to the size necessary for birth.

Naturally, as the source of all life, men were revered. This ancient "scientific" view fit nicely into the strong patriarchal culture in which men were the center of social and religious life. Like many ancient patriarchal cultures, the ancient Hebrews viewed women not only as second-class citizens but actually of a different order altogether, lives worthy of ownership and use by men.

The movement away from this patriarchal world begins in the earliest chapters of our scriptures. Both creation accounts that come to us through our Jewish forebears in Genesis say something radical for their time. Both stories, in different ways, place men and women next to each other, either by treating them together ("He created them male and female") or making a clear biological connection between the bodies of men and the bodies of women (Adam's rib).

In Jesus, God once more confronts patriarchal cultural and religious attitudes. Women, before viewed only as valuable property subject to the will of their owner-husbands, were seen by Jesus as human beings worthy of respect. In his discourses with the Pharisees about divorce, Jesus continued to drive this point home. Even more profound is Jesus' friendship and valuing of women in his ministry. In spite of Paul's early teachings on family life, the early church clearly began to count women among its leadership.

Today, two millenia later, we still struggle with patriarchy. In spite of ourselves, many of us continue to hold the status of men above the status of women. Nothing has illuminated this for me more than my own transition from the social role of male to female. During the first few months after I began living full-time as a female, I had a problem bumping into people. At first, I thought it was simply a kind of emotional dizziness

11

that had come from finally allowing myself full expression of my true identity. However, I began to notice that my collisions were almost exclusively with men.

It took much self-analysis before I realized that men and women navigate public spaces differently. Men tend to walk directly toward their destination, and women tend toward the more circuitous route. I realized suddenly one day, after another such collision (again with a man), that men take precedence over women in public space. The same man who might hold open a door for me in one situation would walk right into me on the sidewalk. I realized that men have the right of way! Having navigated most of my life as a man, I simply was navigating like a man in public while men were expecting me to navigate like a woman. Hence, we collided!

My entire life has been filled with the struggle, often with God, about the difference between what I looked like, how I was treated by others, and what I felt like on the inside. My own patriarchal feelings contributed to my sense that it was somehow shameful that I felt like a woman and wanted desperately to be one. I knew for certain that I would become a miserable outcast were I ever to reveal my terrible truth.

Yet, throughout history, God has been calling people away from the ancient myth that men and women are somehow of different substance and therefore profoundly different from each other. God has continued to lead us away from the prejudice and ignorance to which we all are victim, toward the light of truth.

The church, an institution so frequently characterized by its strong patriarchy (in spite of being the Bride of Christ), has entered a time when it must truly face the reformation of gender as we have known it. My request that the church recognize my transgender reality comes at a time when we as the church are disoriented by our own experience of being transgender— of collectively shifting from patriarchy and control by men toward embracing gender equality and women in leadership.

As people of faith continue to come to terms with the experiences of transgender people—and the many different varieties of gender expression in our midst—there will be challenges ahead. Many welcoming churches have casually added the "T" to their public statements of inclusivity for lesbian, gay, and bisexual people, without realizing that the issues raised by transgender people are different in many ways. Churches that have learned to tolerate differences in the expressions of affection that occur in the privacy of the bedroom may find it more difficult to understand and accept public expressions of ourselves that do not match their cultural expectations.

Questions about gender—and the deeply held myths that surround it—are certain to raise fear and anger within the church. We are accustomed to minding our bodies; we are much less comfortable embodying our minds. Transgender reality calls this into question and may become the center of a struggle in the years to come.

The truth that transgender people live out in our lives is a truth that the people of God are struggling to understand. I have never really been a man, and I know I can never really be a woman in the same way that cisgender women are. I am a transgender woman and will always remain so. My hope is that the church, too, will recognize its transgender nature and discover more fully God's love for us all—not because we are male or female (or anything in between), but because we are all God's children.

Notes

The Reverend Erin K. Swenson, Th.M., Ph.D., was ordained as Eric Karl Swenson in 1973 by the Presbytery of Atlanta, which was then a part of the southern Presbyterian Church in the U.S. Twenty-three years later in 1996, after completing a gender transition, that ordination was upheld by the Presbytery of Greater Atlanta, PCUSA, making Erin the first known mainline clergyperson to transition from male to female while remaining in ordained office.

This article was originally published in *The Other Side* magazine, Volume 37, Number 3 (May–June 2001). It was updated for this anthology.

Suggested scripture

Genesis 2:18–25—Adam and Eve Created (see Chapter 7 of *OtherWise Christian*)

Luke 10:38–42—Mary and Martha of Bethany (see Chapter 24 of *OtherWise Christian*)

John 4—Disciples Surprised by Jesus Talking to a Woman

For further reflection

How have you been shaped by the idea that men and women are fundamentally different?

How are sexual orientation and gender identity different? How are they similar?

In what ways might we consider the church itself to be transgender? How has gender changed in the church during your lifetime? Does gender seem like an important religious issue to you?

Holy Week

By Cameron Partridge

And here we offer and present unto thee, O Lord,
our selves, our souls and bodies,
to be a reasonable, holy, and living sacrifice unto thee;
humbly beseeching thee that
we, and all others who shall be partakers
of this Holy Communion,
may worthily receive
the most precious Body and Blood
of thy Son Jesus Christ,
be filled with thy grace
and heavenly benediction,
and made one body with him,
that he may dwell in us,
and we in him.

Book of Common Prayer, 336

Week by week from about seventh grade through high school, I listened intently to the (above) prayer in the Episcopal parish in which I grew up. Something about these words particularly captured my attention. In them, all of us gathered in worship were offering ourselves in gratitude for the saving work of God in Jesus Christ. Through them, we prayed to receive the holy gifts of bread and wine, body and blood, with reverence to be made one body with Christ, "that he might dwell in us, and we in him." That language of bodily oneness and mutual indwelling moved me deeply.

Yet, at the same time, an insistent question swirled in my head: What does it mean to present one's *body* to God as a vessel, a living instrument of praise? Lifting up my soul somehow felt less complicated. It was the inclusion of body in this equation that muddled it.

I had long lived with a strong sense of disjunction between how I experienced my gender and how the world gendered me as someone assigned female at birth. On top of that disconnect, I felt guilty about how I felt. By adolescence, the experience was intensifying. Kneeling in the sanctuary as a young acolyte, trying to join in that prayer, I stumbled over that phrase of bodily offering. How could I offer a body from which I felt so disconnected?

While that phrase, "our selves, our souls and bodies," stayed with me throughout high school, it faded from memory during college and my first years of divinity school. The churches I attended used different Eucharistic prayers. Then, my partner gave me a book that happened to be titled *Our Selves, Our Souls and Bodies.* On the inside cover she had written, "that you may come to better understand and integrate all the wonderful parts of you!" The volume had been published to address the then-current (mid-1990s) state of the Episcopal Church's sexuality wars. Since I had come out as gay in college and since I had been exploring a sense of call to a combination of ordained ministry and scholarship since my teens, the book's topic was of particular interest to me. As I read the title, that old phrase sounded back into my head like a bell.

For several years, I had been reading feminist, gender, and queer theoretical and theological reflections on embodiment. While plenty of what I had read along the way resonated with my experience, it also often implied that the answer to a disconnect such as mine lay in embracing my body as it was. And so, I continued to wonder: How can I give thanks for and offer up a body from which I felt persistently disconnected? Especially during my first years of divinity school, that feeling hung over my life like a dense fog.

Several years later, as a candidate for ordination to the priesthood, I brought this struggle to my spiritual director—a wise, patient woman who spent an hour with me each week in prayer and reflection. She had been totally nonplussed by my revelation that I had come to view myself as transgender. I told her that I was not sure how I was called to embody my gender. I just knew that I wanted spiritual direction to help me make sense of my gender journey, to invite God consciously into it, and to cultivate an awareness of how God was already at work in it. Not only had she been totally accepting, she had seemed downright pleased to be working with me around this topic.

Yet, when she raised the issue of embodiment, I tensed up and held my breath. I was concerned that certain well-worn paths of bodily interpretation (often termed "essentialist") were going to be imposed on me as they had been so many times before. I listened carefully as she read from a poem that included the following lines:

> I ask God for a special kind of body and get the one I have right now. What thoughts and feelings do I have about this body? ... My relationship with my body powerfully affects my life for good or evil. The finest way to heal, or deepen, the relationship is dialogue. My body must be frank in

expressing its resentments—and its fears—of me. I must be just as frank. ... Scripture reveals my body's spirituality. It says my body is God's temple, the spirit's dwelling place. What does that mean? It further says our bodies are not ours but Christ's, so he can say of me, "This is my body." (excerpt, "The Vessel" by Anthony De Mello, S.J.)

As I listened, I noticed the open, inquiring spirit of the words. What is my attitude toward my body, and where did I get it? A fine question, I thought. My relationship with my body certainly does affect the rest of my life, for good or ill. No doubt about it.

The line about my body needing to be "frank in expressing its resentments—and its fears—of me" also struck a chord. I can still hear her voice, clear as day, reading the line, "I must be just as frank."

Finally, this question about what it means for my body to be God's temple reverberated through me. Indeed, what might it mean for Christ to say of me with all my ambiguity and questions, "This is my body"?

Speaking to God about my long-standing experience of bodily disconnection was long overdue on my part. This poem became a wellspring to which I repeatedly returned. Why were questions of embodiment such a stumbling block for me? What was I to make of my experience of disjuncture from this body, this temple of the Holy? Where was the Spirit in the midst of it all?

Often, I sensed the Spirit in the words and actions of others, in reading, in listening, or in relating—but, not in my body. That was not a fact of which I was proud—especially since I was aware of rich contributions being made to Christian theology, particularly by feminist theologians, concerning the intersection of bodies, the erotic, and God.

Gregory of Nyssa's concept of *epektasis*, a process of constantly stretching forth in desire toward God, and of God expanding our capacity for the divine, had also struck a chord with me along the way. I had begun to feel that, whatever process of stretching toward God may have been afoot in my life, it was entangled with my gender and how I embodied it. I did not understand how. I simply reached a point when I knew without a doubt that I needed a new relationship with my body.

Tectonic plates had long been moving beneath the surface of my everyday life. Pressure was building up and had to be alleviated. As I prayed and reflected on this pressure, one potential action, one route toward embracing my body kept surfacing within me, inviting inquiry: chest surgery. The possibility of actually having a relatively flat chest resonated strongly with me. Intuitively, in my gut, it felt very right. Nevertheless, I was also ambivalent.

In previous years, I had researched chest surgery as a possibility. I had become overwhelmed by the likelihood that my chest would have scars.

17

As I sat with that reaction, I had to ask myself what that was about. What did such scars represent to me? Initially, I think they spoke to me of what a significant surgery this could be, what a major change this procedure would make to my own body. Bodily transformation is not something I have ever taken lightly. I have never even dyed my hair. For me to consider such a change was major.

Somewhere along the way, I had also received the message that trans people who engage in medical transition are rejecting our bodies and turning away from our own creation. I consciously rejected that message, but it still sank in enough to amplify whatever internalized transphobia I was carrying.

I also had hesitations about engaging medical transition because of how its processes have been regulated historically, reinforcing oppressive patterns of sexism, heterosexism, and rigidly binary ideas of gender. Because insurance would not cover transition-related medical procedures at that time, I also was going to have to get a loan. I recognized the privilege involved in all of this, from accessing medical care, to getting a loan, to being able to pay it back.

Over time, sifting through these various reactions, critiques, and wonderings, I continued to ponder chest surgery and scars. Scars can bear witness to pain and even to a certain kind of death. Yet, scars are also signs of healing and witnesses to survival. They do not erase what has gone before but are markers of passage, witnessing to life in its pain and complexity.

This is where the Christian concept of the Paschal Mystery came in for me. That Mystery is the story of the death and resurrection of Jesus Christ—of new life emerging out of death. The body of the resurrected Christ is a living, breathing body, which is marked by and alive to its own history, yet also unchained by it. This mystery began to assist and hold my discernment process. How might my own scars, past, present, and future, emotional and physical, enable me truly to experience my body as my own? As God's own? As part of what the Apostle Paul called the Body of Christ?

The chest reconstruction that I was contemplating would likely leave scars just beneath the curve of pectoral muscles. Under each armpit would also be some sort of mark where drains would empty fluid for some days after surgery. Depending on how healing unfolded, these lines might be thick or thin, prominent or barely visible.

As I pondered these likely scars, an image came into my mind from an art history course years earlier: a small, ivory carving by the so-called Echternacht Master called "Doubting Thomas" (approximately 1000 CE). It depicts a moment in the Gospel of John when the resurrected Jesus invites a skeptical Thomas to believe that a resurrected, living Jesus truly stands before him. "Put your finger here and see my hands" Jesus invites him. "Reach out your hand and put it in my side. Do not doubt but believe" (John 20:27 NRSV). My textbook described the carving in this way:

> Thomas explores the wound in Christ's side in a kind of climbing, aggressive curiosity. Christ, his right arm raised to reveal his side, bends over Thomas in an attitude that wonderfully combines gentleness, benign affection, protectiveness, and sorrow. (*Gardner's Art Through the Ages: Ancient, Medieval and Non-European Art*, eighth edition)

What originally moved me about this image, including its description, was the vulnerability of Jesus in allowing Thomas to "explore" his side. Now, something else struck me: the fact that Jesus' death is not smoothed over in this resurrection appearance. Jesus is revealed not only as risen, but specifically as one who had previously lived and died—whose very body remained marked by those experiences.

The marks of that suffering and death in Christ's risen body have been important sites of reflection for Christians. Early on, Christian art seemed to avoid depicting Jesus' death in crucifixion imagery. Yet, by the Middle Ages, Jesus's wounds were routinely and prominently displayed. In these depictions, the wound on the side of Jesus' body would often stand out as a red half-moon.

Medieval Cistercian theologian Bernard of Clairvaux wrote about that wound as part of a series of homilies on the Song of Songs. The medieval anchorite and mystical theologian Julian of Norwich also reflected upon Jesus' scars as a sign of the nourishing, ultimately creative role Christ plays in the lives of those who love him. These reflections were part of a larger ascetic theological archive that could engage gender in ways surprisingly ambiguous and transformative, even as they could also be oppressively restrictive.

In the midst of this time of study and discernment, I was driving down the highway one day when all at once the thought popped into my head that chest surgery scars can remarkably resemble some medieval depictions of Jesus' side wound. I laughed out loud. Then as I continued to drive and reflect, I felt something clicking into place. I felt surrounded, carried by an expansive sense of the collective Body of Christ. I suddenly knew there was room for me in this Body. My own body could be and was even then already embraced by that wider Body. I was not yet ready, but I knew in that moment that I would have chest surgery someday.

A year later, I was ready to put a date on the calendar. I called up the office of the surgeon with whom I had been corresponding and inquired about the possibility of having surgery over my spring break. It would be difficult, given the limited recovery time, but it could work, they said. I was determined, so we chose a date.

After hanging up the phone, I looked at my calendar more closely and I could not believe it: the date turned out to be in the middle of Holy Week, the holiest week of the Christian calendar, leading up to Easter. Again, I just had to laugh.

In the next moment, I realized this coincidence would allow me to use Lent to prepare for this momentous step. I had taken up other projects for Lent in the past. The first time I observed Lent, as a teen, I had given up chocolate. Another year, I had set out to carve my own version of the Jesus/Thomas interchange (I never finished). This year I would be giving up… (let's just say my bishop was not as amused by this as I was).

The weeks flew by as I prepared for surgery. I talked with people who had been through it. I tried to eat healthily and sleep well, and not to be consumed by the stress of all that was going on in my life. At the beginning of Holy Week, I flew to California where my partner then lived and where the surgeon was located.

That Wednesday at dawn, we drove to the hospital, and hours later I was wheeled into surgery. Soon, the anesthesiologist came in, and, then, in what seemed like the next moment, I was in the recovery room. It was actually done! I felt such a sense of relief.

The next evening was Maundy Thursday. I made my way to church with my chest tightly bound. Worship on this night recalls Jesus' "last supper"—when at the table with his disciples Jesus asked that they break bread and drink wine to remember him. "This is my body given for you; my blood shed for you" he said, and we repeat every time we partake of this gift. Hearing that message in that moment, I felt again that powerful sense of embrace in Christ's collective Body.

Good Friday worship featured a Stations of the Cross to mark this most solemn of days in the church year. The day's emphasis on the radical solidarity of God with humanity in the depths of pain and suffering has long moved me. I was glad to make my way reflectively around the stations on this day, and grateful to be in much less pain than the day before. Admittedly, I also was getting a bit stir crazy and goofy: my partner and I managed to lose it quietly over the typo we found in a station that featured a meditation on "perfectionism."

By Easter Sunday, I could barely contain my joy. The sermon especially resonated. Easter is not something we simply observe like a movie or remember as a past event that is over and done with, the preacher said. It is a mystery in which we *participate* every day throughout our lives. Sitting in the back row among a gaggle of squirmy kids, jelly beans flying overhead, that message hit home.

As I received communion a few minutes later, hearing "the Body of Christ, the Bread of Heaven," I could not stop myself from responding,

"Participant!"

A week later, the first Sunday after Easter, I was back in Massachusetts in my sponsoring congregation. This is always the day when the story of Thomas' encounter with Jesus is assigned in the lectionary. As I listened to the familiar gospel passage that morning, thinking of that ivory carving, the words, "Reach out your hand and put it in my side. Do not doubt but believe," brought me full circle.

For me, this was a Holy Week like never before. I felt truly embraced by the Paschal Mystery. I knew myself to be a member of Christ's Body, a partaker of it, a participant in it. Finally, I felt able to offer my whole life, my whole self, to God.

In the words of the letter to the Ephesians, "Glory to God whose power, working in us, can do infinitely more than we can ask or imagine" (*Book of Common Prayer*, page 102, based on Ephesians 3:20–21).

Notes

The Reverend Dr. Cameron Partridge is an Episcopal priest, theologian, and openly trans and genderqueer-identified man. He came out as trans during his ordination process and was ordained a deacon in 2004 and a priest in 2005 in the Episcopal Diocese of Massachusetts. Since then he has served in parish, campus ministry, and university/divinity school settings. In 2016, he and his family moved to California where he now serves as the Rector of St. Aidan's Episcopal Church in San Francisco, California. He and his spouse have two children.

This essay first appeared in *Crossing Paths: Where Transgender and Religion Meet* (2003), edited by Mr. Barb Greve, published by the Unitarian Universalist Association. Abridged and revised for this anthology.

The opening prayer is from *The Book of Common Prayer* (New York: Church Hymnal Corporation, 1979), page 336. *Our Selves, Our Souls and Bodies: Sexuality and the Household of God* (Cowley Publications, 1996) was edited by Charles Hefling. The poem excerpt is from "The Vessel" by Anthony De Mello, S.J., in *Wellsprings: A Book of Spiritual Exercises* (Doubleday & Company, Inc., 1985), pages 23–24. The referenced Easter sermon was delivered by the Reverend Matthew McDermott at St. Mark's Episcopal Church in Palo Alto, California, in 2003.

The reference to *epektasis* comes from Gregory of Nyssa, *The Life of Moses* (Paulist Press, 1978) translated by Abraham J. Malherbe and Everett Ferguson, pages 111–120. The author was introduced to the topic by several teachers along the way, but especially by Sarah Coakley. She writes about this topic in *Powers and Submission: Spirituality, Philosophy and Gender* (Blackwell, 2002).

The Jesus/Thomas image was on page 336 of *Gardner's Art Through the Ages: Ancient, Medieval and Non-European Art,* eighth edition (Harcourt Brace Jovanovich, Publishers, 1986) by Horst de la Croix and Richard G. Tansey. Bernard of Clairvaux reflects on the side wound in Homily #61 of *The Sermons on the Song of Songs, Volume III* (Cistercian Publications/Liturgical Press, 1979); Julian of Norwich does so in *Revelations of Divine Love* (Penguin Books, 1998). Scholarship the author encountered on gender and the side wound when first writing this piece included Caroline Bynum, *Jesus As Mother: Studies in the Spirituality of the High Middle Ages* (University of California Press, 1984) and *Fragmentation and Redemption* (Zone Books, 1991).

On gender and embodiment in early Christian asceticism, the author was particularly influenced by Diana Swancutt and Ellen Aitken with whom he studied between 2000 and 2002.

Suggested scripture

John 20:19–29—Jesus and Thomas (see the Epilogue of *OtherWise Christian*)

1 Corinthians 12:27 and Romans 12:4–5—The Body of Christ

Ephesians 3:20–21—Glory to God

For further reflection

Are you able to offer up your whole self to God? What does that mean to you?

Do you experience your body as part of the wider Body of Christ?

How do you make meaning out of your scars (literal or figurative)?

OtherWise

By Chris Paige

But he himself insisted,
"I am who I am."

John 9:9b
author's translation

As I sit in church watching my friend Paul preside over communion, I am moved to tears.

Paul and I were both Presbyterians. After finishing Princeton Seminary as an out gay man, Paul joined a congregation that was aligned with both the United Church of Christ (UCC) and the Presbyterian Church (U.S.A.). I joined the same church a few years later. That is where we met and became friends.

Despite Paul's gifts for ministry, the Presbyterian Church would not ordain him because he is openly gay. The dually-aligned status of our congregation presented him with a choice and an invitation: He could stay in the Presbyterian Church, which was his home, but where he could not fulfill his calling, or he could transfer his affiliation to the UCC and pursue ordination.

After much soul-searching, Paul decided to pursue ordination. I remember vividly the day he was ordained as a UCC minister and presided over the Lord's Supper that first time. The emotion was palpable. It was a moment of both joy and grief as Paul stepped forth into this new identity.

It is several years later. Now as I watch him in this, his not-so-new church, far from where I first met him, he says the words of institution as nonchalantly as if he had been saying them all his life. I weep tears of joy at seeing him, after so many years of struggle, fulfilling his call. He has survived the difficult choice to leave the church he was raised in, where he found his faith, and he has made a new home.

I know many other lesbian and gay ministers and seminary graduates who have been faced with a similar choice and decided to stay in their denomination of origin to work for reconciliation. Each has a unique story. They are prophets and ministers of transformation in a church that often seems it would be just as happy without them.

And then there is me—and others like me. I am both in and out of the Presbyterian Church. I claim this "both-and," caught somewhere in between.

I care deeply about the Presbyterian Church and its struggles. I remain a member of a local Presbyterian congregation, serve as an elder, and regularly participate in the life of the church. But, I have also left the Presbyterian Church. I no longer attend Presbytery meetings. I keep national church politics and the struggle to reshape the Presbyterian Church at arm's length. I am wary of identifying myself too much as Presbyterian. That identity feels like a trap that holds me in an embattled state of being, unable to be "home."

Yet, I do not have it in me to abandon my church tradition and identify with the UCC or some other more affirming church body—though I could easily do so without even leaving my local church. I am somewhere in-between, neither in nor out. I live at the margins of each identity while seeking to be at the center of myself. I have let go of the idea that the Presbyterian Church is capable of holding my full spiritual identity.

These struggles and choices mirror my dilemma around gender identity. I was assigned a female identity at birth, but I have come to realize that this identity has created substantive internal conflict for me. No matter how I have tried to reconstruct "woman," it still feels limiting—as if it somehow cuts off an important part of me.

I will always be a woman in the same ways that I will always be a Presbyterian. Both of these affiliations have shaped me into who I am in important ways. Meanwhile, I am also letting go of the idea that "woman" is capable of holding my full gender identity. I am freeing myself to explore my own inclinations and leadings without feeling any pressure to justify them in terms of a "female" identity.

Certainly "man" is another option. I am sometimes mistaken for a man and could blend in pretty well as male, especially if I worked at it. I have seriously considered whether that label fits me better than "woman." However, it is just not who I am. I may be male by association in some circumstances, by the structures and traditions of our society, but I do not feel it is my journey to become a transsexual man. For me, such a transition would not solve my dilemma—in the same way that actively identifying with the United Church of Christ would not bring me home. It is simply not who I am.

I am somewhere in between—not really male, not completely comfortable as female. I am OtherWise. I appear to live on the cusp of indecision—but only because we are all taught to demand a decision.

It was when I began to read the work of Kate Bornstein, author of *Gender Outlaw* and *My Gender Workbook*, that I began to let go of the struggle to fit into male or female boxes. I was able to name the insidious societal violence I experienced growing up as a child, a violence that I call "nonconsensual gender."

Most of us are assigned a gender at birth. This label—typically male or female—goes on to define nearly every interaction we have as children and adults. We are taught that this identity is permanent, immutable, and nonnegotiable.

Some of us—and this is my experience—enter a social world where the expectations associated with this label terrorize us. The pressure to conform is constant. We are expected to cut off parts of ourselves in order to fit into binary boxes: either male or female. In addition, we are expected to graft on pieces of identity that feel utterly foreign to us—further threatening our integrity. This pressure is applied through threat, command, and outright hostility, as well as through systematic but nuanced forms of reaction, rejection, disapproval, abandonment, and lack of support.

This subtle violence leaves its mark. The violence and terrorism of nonconsensual gender begins so early, however, that we hardly "remember" it. It has always been part of the fabric of our lives. We grow accustomed to this ever-present force. Our adaptations become unconscious habits.

Personally, I was raised to be a little feminist. I had been told from early on that I could be anything I wanted. This understanding empowered me in a variety of ways—from playing with toy cars instead of Barbies to being good at math and science and sports. I always had unconditional support at home. Nonetheless, at a some level, both conscious and unconscious, I learned that there were also gender limits and expectations.

The message of conformity came to me in many subtle and not-so-subtle ways. When I was done playing in the dirt with the boys, I would have to line up with the pretty girls in dresses, reminding me that I did not fit in either world. The boys on my middle school basketball team blatantly refused to pass me the ball—even after I scored three-quarters of our points! Recognition of achievements was sometimes noted with reference to my gender. Returning my outstanding work on several science papers, my otherwise progressive high school teacher joked, "Nobody likes a smart girl." Whether for kindergarten plays or college basketball team travel, there was a social expectation that I wear a dress.

Social cues taught me that it was not acceptable to "be whatever I wanted to be." I learned to watch my step and made constant choices between conforming to or resisting the gender expectations of those around me.

As an adult, when store clerks call me "sir" and then recognize their mistake, I find the intensity of their anxiety confounding. As a child I was often mistaken for a boy, and such negative reactions, experienced regularly, communicated a great deal to me about the impropriety of my identity. In fact, I wore long hair from middle school through college specifically to avoid that experience. Such adaptations helped me survive, but they also threatened my integrity.

Through careful presentation and social awareness, I somehow attempted to reconcile these two radically opposite notions—that I was both pure potentiality and that I was deeply wrong. On the surface, I guess I made it work, but the dissonance I experienced cut deep. My subconscious learned well what society taught me through years of interactions and assumptions and expectations and reactions. I know now that simplistic labels do not fit the complexity of our actual identities.

Having identified myself as a survivor of this systemic, societal abuse, I am now empowered to explore my gender identity from a fresh position, rejecting both "male" and "female." Instead I claim "OtherWise" as my gender identity. In that process, I am slowly growing more aware of the pieces of myself that I attempted to cut off in order to survive—the "boy" parts and the "girl" parts that were pitted against one another. I am learning to put the pieces back together in new ways. I am a survivor of the violence and terrorism of nonconsensual gender, but I am no longer divided against myself.

Only now, from a place of growing wholeness, can I question more deeply the assumptions that forced me to make such agonizing choices, as if the world would fall apart if I remained suspended somewhere above or between the two limited options of male or female. We are taught that it is essential to be one or the other. You are either in the Presbyterian Church or not. You are either male or female. You have one and only one identity, and the lines are allegedly clear. Well, I refuse to make that choice. To do so would do violence to myself. It would violate the fullness of all that is me.

Instead, I claim my place as OtherWise—and this is the OtherWisdom that I bring: that we do not have to choose, that "either-or" is not the only option, that this place of "both-and" is one of joy and fullness—even as it brings new grief and struggle. I bring you this OtherWisdom—that your own integrity must define your identity. For some this will mean continuing to identify with the gender (or church) you were assigned at birth, while shaping and reshaping that tradition and what it means to you as you change and grow and make visible your deepest self.

For others, the choice will be different. Erin Swenson left behind the gender identity she was assigned at birth in order that she might live fully in her identity as a woman. This is similar to my friend Paul who left behind the church tradition of his birth to live fully in his identity as a UCC minister. Paul's early life as a Presbyterian will forever affect his identity and his story—but he is now fully a member of the United Church of Christ. Similarly, while Erin is forever influenced by her early life presenting as a man, she is now fully identified as a woman.

In each case, there is a transition, a change in identity. The person inside is basically the same—but the individual makes a choice, a change, in order to live with more integrity and honesty. Then, there are the rest of us—those who refuse to choose. I choose to stay suspended somewhere in between. I do not correct people when they mistake me for a man. Yet, if forced to choose, I identify as a woman because it seems safer, all things considered.

Still, something deep inside of me is set free when I say both (or neither). When I claim this label "OtherWise," I experience a fullness of spirit that brings with it a powerful sense of joy and wholeness. There are these two parts of myself (that is, "masculine" and "feminine") that have long been in conflict with each other. In OtherWise, they make peace, join hands, and begin to dance.

I do not know yet all that this new identification will mean for me, but I am sure of this one thing: Each of us has a gift to bring when we live with integrity. Yet, we can discover the full nature of that gift only when we actually live in a way that is authentic to who we are.

Our choices will surely vary. Identities may shift with time. But, together, we weave a story of healing, which joins with others throughout the centuries. Like the blind man in John's Gospel who was asked to explain his healing and new identity, let us testify to our own integrity and sing out along with the One in whose image we have been created: "I am who I am" (John 9:9b, author's translation).

Notes

Mx Chris Paige is the author of *OtherWise Christian: A Guidebook for Transgender Liberation* (2019) and the editor of this anthology. Mx Chris now uses they/them pronouns. They were the publisher of *The Other Side* magazine in 2001 when this article first appeared (together with the Mollenkott and Swenson reflections). Learn more at http://www.chrispaige.com.

This article was originally published in *The Other Side* magazine, Volume 37, Number 3 (May–June 2001). It was updated for publication in this anthology, but describes non-binary gender identity at a time before "non-binary" had been adopted as a commonly used term.

Kate Bornstein's *Gender Outlaw: On Men, Women and the Rest of Us* was originally published in 1995, but a revised and updated version came out in 2016. A sequel anthology, called *Gender Outlaws: The Next Generation* was published in 2010. Her *Gender Workbook: How to Become a Real Man, a Real Woman, the Real You, or Something Else Entirely* was published in 1998. The second edition was re-titled as *My New Gender Workbook: A Step-by-Step Guide to Achieving World Peace Through Gender Anarchy and Sex Positivity* in

2013.

　As of 2018, Presbyterian Church (U.S.A.) policy allows for the full-participation of both same-gender-loving and transgender people, though cultural change is still needed. Meanwhile, Paige has become more and more involved in the United Church of Christ since writing this reflection some 19 years ago. They remain a member at the dually aligned church but also worship and serve in another Philadelphia area congregation. They have lived out their "both-and" calling in a variety of ecumenical and multi-faith ministry roles.

Suggested scripture

　Exodus 3—Moses Receives God's Name, "I Am," at the Burning Bush (see Chapter 1 of *Christian Faith and Gender Identity* by Mx Chris Paige)

　John 8:58—Jesus as "I Am"

　John 9:1–12—Blind Man Healed (and Testifies "I Am")

For further reflection

　What do we lose, as a community, when individuals are asked to live inauthentically?

　Paige describes "the violence of non-consensual gender." How can gender be consensual?

　How might you show up differently if you were able to live into the "fullness of all that is [you]"? Are there parts of you that remain hidden?

Every Body Is Good. You're Welcome.

By Donovan Ackley III

> *So God created* [the adam] *in his own image,*
> *in the image of God he created them;*
> *male and female he created them.*

Genesis 1:27 NIV

In early 2013, I was still presenting publicly as the typical Christian wife of a typical Christian husband. I made headline news when I came out as transgender, after taking the name Adam, and embracing a masculine gender presentation. However, the deeper and more wonderful story is that I am (and have always been) intersex.

At the time of my gender transition, I had not yet received an accurate medical diagnosis, so "transgender" was the best language that I had to talk about my experience. Like many other intersex people, I had struggled with serious health concerns and had been confused about what was happening with my body for a very long time.

Since puberty, I had been fighting my God-given gender identity with medical and psychopharmaceutical interventions, as well as prayer and therapy. Up to this point, I had been trying to work with the doctors and counselors who were trying to make me into a "proper" woman, but the wrongly prescribed medications and side effects had nearly killed me.

Finally at the age of 47, the doctors ordered me to stop fighting— and as a result, I quickly changed from being a mentally-ill woman to being a sane and increasingly healthy transgender man.

During that season, as I quietly recovered during a sabbatical from teaching ministry, theology, and church history at Azusa Pacific University, I was delighted to find out that even then-83-year-old conservative evangelical televangelist Pat Robertson, host of the Christian Broadcasting Network's *The 700 Club*, had just publicly acknowledged that, though it happens only rarely, some of us identify with genders that seem counter to our own bodies and that this is not a sin to be condemned. Only God can know and judge such things about each of us. At that point, it seemed that evangelical Christians did not have any particular opinion on gender minorities.

In even the most conservative communities of faith where I have worshiped, practiced, and taught, everyone seemed to believe that everyone, without exception, is created in the image of God (Genesis 1:27–28). To understand what it means to be created in God's image, we affirm that our Creator understands us intimately, as God told the Hebrew prophet Jeremiah: "Before I formed you in the womb, I knew you" (Jeremiah 1:5, NIV).

In that spirit, when my pastor asked me to preach during her summer vacation, I was filled with hope. While ours was a progressive church that affirmed same-sex couples, gender issues had not yet explicitly been addressed. With my pastor's encouragement, I prepared to preach a sermon on gender diversity, originally titled "The Genderqueer Gospel" (a message of inclusion for others like me). By the time I preached the sermon, it had become "God's Good News for *All* People" (a message to the *whole* Church that including gender minorities is liberating for us all).

This congregation had been so good to me and my children for more than a decade—especially in my times of serious illness. I very much wanted this message to be good news for *them*. So, my focus was on preaching the gospel message of God's boundless grace to the majority of people in the congregation—those who were not only neither trans nor intersex, but not even gay, lesbian, or bisexual.

The pain of being forced to live in bondage to human-created ideas about gender that do not fit us can be especially sharp for many of us who are gender minorities (especially in conservative faith communities), but, surely, it is a challenge that faces each and every one of us to varying degrees. I wanted to ask them generally, "What do people who are 'gender nonconforming' need from God and from those of us who love and follow Jesus?"

This was my first sermon preaching as Adam—the first time I had preached at all in years and the first time I had shared my ministry gifts with this congregation. As much as I wanted to preach for everyone, I also needed to admit that this question was never going to be purely theological or pastoral for me. It was also confessional. While I did not set out to prepare a "coming out" sermon, I did resolve that, in order to walk in integrity with my church family, I needed to be truthful about what this topic meant to me.

"I AM" is the personal name God uses with Moses in Exodus 3:14 (at the burning bush) and one of the seven core biblical names of God in Jewish tradition. To be created in God's image means to share God's likeness—to be able to say of oneself, simply, "I am!" (just as God did when Moses asked for God's name).

During my sabbatical and preparation for that sermon, I found out that GLAAD, the American organization that monitors and guides media representation of LGBTQ people, named a new campaign, "I Am: Trans People Speak." The campaign highlighted transgender stories. The power of this connection hit me like a punch in the gut. Yes, even transgender people are made in the image of God. Every time we say "Yes, I am," we invoke the name of God, the very Being of the One who made us: I AM. We are. We exist. We exist because the great "I AM" made us.

Still, what exactly does it mean to affirm that each of us is created in God's image? In the first biblical story of creation (Genesis 1), the human being is created both individual and plural. "God created the human being in God's own image. ... male and female God created them" (Genesis 1:27, author's translation). The word *adam* in Hebrew is a collective word. It is not a proper name. *H'adam* (the human) simply means one hand-crafted by God from *adamah* (the clay or dust of the ground) and brought to life by the breath of God's own Spirit. I took the name "Adam" in order to claim myself as such a creature.

The next version of the creation story (Genesis 2) is even more explicit that God creates humankind to be in community: God recognizes that it is not good for that first human to be *alone* but that they needed to have companionship and partnership. The one flesh of the *adam* is then divided into two equal beings, gendered now as woman and man.

All of us were created by God. Each of us is fully human though we may be different in a variety of ways, including gender. Whatever we look like, whatever we may think of each other, we are *all* equally fearfully and wonderfully crafted by our loving Creator. We all need the same things from God and from one another. We need solidarity with God and with other people.

The sermon went well, though soon afterwards, I lost my job at the university. Over the next four years, I stopped taking the synthetic estrogen and progesterone I had been on for most of 32 years. I started a therapeutic dose of testosterone. The results were atypical and led to a new diagnosis—that I had been born with an intersex condition. It turns out that, no matter what hormones I take, my body tends outwardly to appear both male and female.

Sometimes, especially when I am interacting with other people with intersex variations, I am grateful that I have a healthy even though unusual body. Many people born with intersex variations are subjected to medically unnecessary surgeries at an early age, which result in all manner of complications, including infertility, loss of sexual feeling, and even diminished lifespans. My challenges did not begin until puberty and the medical interventions that I faced were less invasive than some that are quite common among those with intersex variations.

After many years of trying with fasting, prayer, and medical interventions to "correct" these atypical features, the body that remains with me now is just as God has designed it. Even so, I have moments when I recoil in disgust at seeing my own intersex body in the mirror after a shower—a body that is not clearly male or female but, rather, appears to be both.

Over these same years, many conservative evangelicals have taken up the issue of trans bodies and clearly rejected non-binary experience. By 2017, several notable evangelical leaders agreed that it is a topic that is worth dividing the church over. They issued "The Nashville Statement," which strongly denounces transgender people and all who support us (though it provides some ambiguous acknowledgement of people with intersex variations).

Around that time, I was starting to lose myself again in despair and those "I am not good enough and never will be" feelings. Yet, seemingly out of nowhere, my heart was filled with a message that overruled my head, as if from a Higher Power:

> Every person is created in God's image—and GOD, too, is neither male nor female! Being created in God's image is GOOD! Every BODY is good! You're welcome.

Remembering that every one of our bodies is fully human, hand-crafted, and in-Spirited by God—remembering that every one of our bodies is good—has freed me from that despair. The unusual parts of my body, the differences in my body are *good*—even those that exclude me from so many parts of the Body of Christ. God did not have to bless or fix the first animals or the first people to *make* them good; God simply noticed that they *are* good—simply because they *are*.

Some Christians do not yet accept that a person who has always tried to conform to their assigned gender can fail at that task. They typically blame me (and others like me) for not trying hard enough or not submitting sufficiently, even though I have both literal and figurative scars to show from my efforts to comply and conform.

I have found freedom in relying on the Bible for clarity about God's infinite creativity and boundless, loving grace. This love goes well beyond the human cultural constraints regarding gender that we so often impose on one another.

For those of us who are gender minorities, God explicitly encourages each one of us—over and against our own self-denying self-doubting tendencies—through the prophet Isaiah: "Do not let the eunuch say, 'Behold, I am a dry tree'"(Isaiah 56:3 NRSV). Rather, God promises that those eunuchs who "hold fast" to the things God loves will receive an enduring name, "better than sons and daughters" (Isaiah 56:4–5 NRSV).

Jesus later invokes these promises to Isaiah as he affirms those he describes as "eunuchs who have been so from birth" (perhaps like myself and others born with intersex variations), those "made eunuchs by others," and those "who have made themselves eunuchs for the sake of the kingdom of heaven" (Matthew 19:12 NRSV). Jesus accepts and affirms all of these variations as blessed.

Through Isaiah and Jesus, God has promised that being a gender minority neither cuts us off from God nor prevents us from bearing good spiritual fruit. Being intersex and/or transgender are *not* conditions to be ashamed of. We do not need to be fearful or to hide these variations. In and through Jesus Christ, the unity embodied in the first undivided human is restored (Galatians 3:28). This unity is also in the Creator God (who uses "They/Them" and "We/Us" pronouns) and in whose image we are made. In other words, we are *free* in Christ to live as *free* people—not bound by gender or any other human limitation.

In the Psalms, the prayer book of the Bible, we praise God's wondrous creativity, expressed in all the diversity of our individual differences and idiosyncrasies. All that is human is praised because God is the Creator of *all* that is:

> You have searched me, Lord, and you know me... For you created my inmost being; you knit me together in my mother's womb. I praise you because I am fearfully and wonderfully made; your works are wonderful, I know that full well. My frame was not hidden from you when I was made in the secret place, when I was woven together in the depths of the earth. Your eyes saw my unformed body.... How amazing are your thoughts concerning me, God! How vast is the sum of them! (Psalm 139:1–17 NIV)

These are just a few of the scriptures that remind me that I am good, just the way that I am. The world continues to tell people with intersex variations that who we are, naturally, is wrong. Yet, God's name is still "I am!" It is in this image of "I AM!" that we are each fearfully and wonderfully made.

Living enslaved to the cultural expectations of others is not required of us in Christ. We are free, even empowered, to be fully ourselves, just as God made us—fully human and so much more than the social roles of gender, race, class, and religion within which we sometimes define and confine each other.

Instead of holding up the harsh mirror of judgment against one another, we can reflect instead God's "I am!" one to another—a Light in which we can each see our own selves as God's beloved more clearly. As each of us declares our own "I am!," we can carefully and deeply embrace God's declaration that each of us is good. God sees all of us. God loves each of us, just as we are!

I was ordained in the Mennonite tradition and the words of this beloved German hymn linger with me still, "God so loved us, and loves me, too. … God … Loves even me." Feeling beloved allows each of us, in turn, to reflect the unbounded Divine Love we have heard and seen back to one another. My prayer is that all of us and all of our children might be offered this confidence—not just to ease our pain and struggle, but because this knowledge is what allows us to welcome one another, just as Jesus taught us.

Notes

The Reverend Dr Donovan Ackley III is a sometimes professor of religious studies with more than three decades of experience in grassroots community organizing and nonviolent conflict resolution, most recently helping to launch the U.S.-Canadian peer support suicide prevention line Trans Lifeline with and for transgender, non-binary, gender nonconforming, and intersex people. He has recently appeared in the documentary film "Intersex and Faith," exploring the intersections of religion and gender.

Ackley received much media attention under the name, "Adam," but over time, he settled on the family name of Donovan. Both names are referenced here with his permission, but Donovan Ackley III should generally be used.

This article draws from Ackley's 2013 "coming out" sermon, "God's Good News for All People," together with his 2017 article, "And It Was Good: A Response to the Nashville Statement." This adaptation incorporates additional insights and understandings that he has gleaned since those offerings.

The GLAAD "I Am" campaign can be found at https://www.glaad.org/transpeoplespeak.

Suggested scripture

Psalm 139—Fearfully and Wonderfully Made

Galatians 3:27–28—No Separation in Christ (see Chapter 22 of *OtherWise Christian*)

Galatians 5—Freedom in Christ

For further reflection

How have you struggled to accept your body?

How have you worked to overcome despair, shame, and self-doubt?

How could this kind of radical intimacy with God who is "I AM" change modern Christian culture?

Holy Hybrid

By Louis Mitchell

*And the Word became flesh
and dwelt among us...*

John 1:14a NRSV

I am a Holy Hybrid—a kaleidoscopic blend of male and female, straight and gay, resourced and poor, educated and self-taught, healthy and disabled, sage and sinner, believer and interrogator, spiritual and carnal, addict and recoverer, youthful and seasoned, sunlight and shadow. My journey to this place of acceptance has had many twists and turns.

When I started using the term, "holy hybrid," it was simply witty wordplay to describe my experience as someone raised as a girl who grew up to be a man. However, as time went by, through experiences, discernment, and growing awareness, it has come to mean so much more to me.

In my tradition, U.S. Protestant Christianity, there is an entrenchment in binary analyses of goodness. We are either "saved" or "sinner." People, things, and ideas are judged to be "of God" or not. These theological ideas align closely with more routine judgments about "in" and "out," about "worthy" and "unworthy" of care.

Sometimes an argument that "we are all sinners" appears, but it typically seems to function more as a matter of convenience, faux humility, or a "get out of jail free" card than a real equalizing impulse in Christian culture. Furthermore, I submit that if God is *the* Creator, then what can possibly be *not* of God?! Theological arguments aside, the concept of "both/and" seems completely lost in much of Christian culture.

Still, I claim this Holy Hybrid space, in the creases and folds *between*, as holy space, as worthy of consideration. More so, I find myself and my people grounded in this kind of space, whether we identify as Christian or not. To be a Holy Hybrid is to claim my own both/and without shame or reservation. To be a Holy Hybrid is to embrace the many layered journeys each one of us must take to find and embrace the gifts that we have been given by our Creator.

I was born on the bubble of life and death in 1960. I was born by caesarian section at 32 weeks (eight weeks premature). I was only four pounds. There was no stretch by the powers that be to provide for extraordinary, life-saving measures for the child of an unwed, poor Black teenager. I spent the first few months of my life in an incubator. I am told that I had a blood clot located near my heart that was surgically removed, but my mom still remembers, with grief and sadness, how poorly she was treated, even as she worried about the health of her only child.

My family dressed me in doll clothes because they could not find clothes small enough to fit me. I was skinny and sickly even through grade school. I was that kid with scarlet fever in Los Angeles in 1970 when such things were unheard of.

I was also told that I was a girl, but by the age of three, I knew that I was something else. Still, I became a good church kid, saved and baptized while still in primary school. So, I did what any faithful person would do. I prayed for God to make me a boy. While praying those many years, I also watched and listened to the people around me. I did not know that I was compiling a dossier on how men and women were supposed to be. I spent my post-puberty years trying to adapt—trying to be a proper female.

I would go on to claim the label of butch lesbian because it was the best language I could find for who and how I was. I know and respect many butches and honor their identities to this day, but I still felt like an imposter trying to fit someone else's script. I soon discovered that gender transition was possible. I was both relieved and afraid.

Those who think that gender transition or even self-affirmation is an effortless decision are just plain ignorant of what it takes. I understand why some people choose self-extermination rather than press through the familial, societal, romantic, medical, political, and religious challenges that are involved. It has not been easy, but it has been worth it. That which had me wanting to die would eventually make me stronger, more open, more alert to gender dynamics and gender essentialist thinking.

I came into my manhood in 1999, beginning medical and legal transition in 2001. I got to take all of the lessons I had compiled through the years and actualize them. I am an intentional man—literally a man on purpose. This does not make me less susceptible to patriarchy and sexism, though I thought that it would. Still, it has made me more open to looking at the ways that unearned privilege serves as a narcotic. It is omnipresent and insidious.

My days and nights of active alcohol and drug abuse unveiled the layers of internalized racism and classism I had ingested growing up in the suburbs. Those days and nights also nearly killed me, so I do not recommend this as a healthy approach to self-awareness, but it was effective. Maybe you can learn from my experience.

In the 'burbs, I was a trouble-making honor student who also abused drugs and alcohol. Once I came of age, my appetite for freebase cocaine took me to the 'hood. In fact, it took me to the exact neighborhood my mom grew up in three decades earlier.

I do not know what it was like before, but I found a mix of mostly Black folk, with a sprinkling of Mexican, Filipino, and some white people—who either could not or would not leave with the rest of the "white flight." There were hard-working families, together with a variety of folk involved in the underground economies of Los Angeles. Some had lost their will to work, getting by with various hustles. Everyone was managing less than ideal circumstances, but there was a deep sense of community amidst these diverse struggles.

I almost blended in, except that I was a super "Erkel." I wore the wrong clothes, spoke the wrong language, and had an utter absence of cool. For years, I had searched for masks to hide my Blackness because I had been taught by the media and even the educational system that we were rioters and malcontents, unworthy recipients of aid, and creators of urban blight.

These misrepresentations cultivated a kind of bigotry covered by an invisible shield of self-loathing. My addiction did not just change my life in awful ways; it also gave me deeper insight into myself and my people. I lived among and partied with people who were fun, kind, and generous. They looked out for each other and for me. They were more open-minded and open-hearted than those I had looked up to in the suburban Black church community of my youth. I am not trying to paint them as super-noble beings who were lacking less than honorable feelings and behaviors found anywhere else. I am just noting that they were not worse than (or better than) any of the white people, middle-class people, or church people I had known.

Confronting my own bias was a formative experience for me. It was during this sojourn in the 'hood that I began deconstructing the binary ways of thinking that I had been taught in church. Even in my addiction, I was learning a lot. I felt so much love for the many ways my people created family, life, and abundance in an economic desert. My newfound pride in these folk helped me to recognize how much harm was being caused by the choices I was making—harm to both me and my community.

In time, I found recovery, returned to organized religion, and found a tug in my spirit toward some type of ministry. I did not want to be a part of church hypocrisy, but I could not resist the pull. Some call their journey to Christian ordination a "calling." I call mine a "dragging."

I had to revisit what I had been taught over and over again about the "sins of the flesh." Early on, I learned that all of the desires of the body should be rejected. It seemed that the body was only to be used as a procreative copy machine without pleasure or desire. Obviously, I disavowed those beliefs during my journey through addiction, but that approach to the body was still ingrained in me and in much of the Christian culture that I would encounter.

But, what is the point of the incarnation, if our bodies are bad? I could not reconcile my up-bringing with the ways our bodies operate, responding to touch, tenderness, and intimacy. I still can't. It matters that God became flesh in Jesus. The Christ child was born of humble beginnings and would go on to be chastised for spending so much time with sinners.

I think that church folk got it wrong. I think that ancient theologians, riddled with guilt and shame, made hard lines where there should not have been any. It does not track for me that a loving and all-knowing God would build us for pleasure just to see how much denial we can withstand. That kind of bitter game-playing behavior sounds decidedly human to me.

So, as I craft my ministry, I chose not to stand in that place of judgment. I reject shame-mongering and the denial of pleasure. I believe that Jesus was, first and foremost, a human Rabbi, with dusty garments and crusty feet. I believe that he experienced hunger, thirst, desire, sadness, joy, hope, and confusion—just like the rest of us. I also believe that Jesus (and all of us) are divine.

It seems that I have best learned the lessons of the Christian faith from looking "up" out of my own humility and brokenness, rather than "down" from the sanctified arrogance of Christian culture. I believe that each one of us can touch, move, heal, restore, and create—just as God intended. I believe that our time on earth has been given in order to see just how much we can find and embrace our gifts. The challenge is to train ourselves to utilize those gifts well and to good purpose—to love and touch those in need and those who are on the margins.

In this both/and place, we are called to be filled with our gifts and to be humble in our giving, to live life as fully as we are able and to share fullness with all whom we encounter. It is in this Holy Hybrid sense of self that we are realized as whole and holy, gift and recipient, broken, healed, and healer.

Notes

The Reverend Louis Mitchell is called to be a conduit to grateful living, a recovery trudger, and ordained clergy with the United Church of Christ.

Suggested scripture

John 1—Prologue to the Gospel of John

Isaiah 7:14—Immanuel

Matthew 1:22–23—Jesus Is "God with Us"

For further reflection

How does dividing people into "good" and "evil" play out in your world? How would things change if you softened the edges of these categories to allow for more complexity in how God moves through us?

How does the "incarnation" impact how you view bodies, touch, tenderness, and intimacy? Do you ever struggle with "sins of the flesh"?

Have you ever been confronted with prejudices that you did not previously realize you had?

Section 2

Resistance and Resilience

Finding Freedom

By Ryan Amir Harris

We know how much God loves us,
and we have put our trust in His love.
God is love,
and all who live in love,
live in God,
and God lives in them.

1 John 4:16 NLT

It was December 2014, at the vigil for high school transgender teen Leelah Alcorn, where I decided to finally live my truth, to live the life that God intended for me to live, a life of integrity. Leelah died by her own hand, leaving behind a suicide note that went viral. In particular, her plea that we "Fix society, please."

I just thought I would meet the media and speak to them regarding what was taking place. As I walked, I reflected on how I got to the vigil— why, as a licensed deacon, I was even asked to attend. I had been asked by a good friend, because the school district where Leelah attended had African-American teens but had no representation of clergy that "looked like" them.

At this point, I was just thinking I was representing the "Black" part of me, but eventually, I realized that I was there to be set free, to stand in my truth, to represent "all" of me.

It was a struggle having multiple identities and being able to live only through the lens of one. It was at this vigil that I decided my life, up until that moment, necessitated a bold move, a lasting imprint on the movement that had just received one of the hardest blows ever—the loss of life.

I needed to be vocal *and* visible because there was no one else in my area talking about being transgender in the Black church or in the Black community. I remembered what it was like not to have the language or a visible "possibility model" there by my side as I matriculated through the phases of my transition, even as an adult.

I was forced to choose: Be Black (African American) or be

transgender. Why not both?! Here I was attending a vigil where a *child* was transitioning and could see *no* hope, received *no* help, and encountered no one with a loving heart for who they were. Children are killing themselves because they can not see anyone like them who is living a productive trans life.

I felt compelled to speak. I was determined to show other trans children and teens who looked like me that they have a right to live out their faith just the way they are. People of faith are not allowed to ridicule someone to the point that death would feel like a relief. Everyone should be able to live out their truth in *love*.

I used the media, the attention in that moment, and the legacy of a beautiful trans teen to scream from the mountain top, "Live free!"

It took a minute for a man, born in a woman's body, raised in the church all my life, to reconcile finally with both my upbringing and the Word of God. It was not an easy task. I went through several phases.

In the beginning, it was easier to be accepted as a lesbian than as a transgender man. At the time, there was no politically correct language for "lesbian." In the vernacular of my church, I functioned as a "dyke." This label was reserved for strong women who wore male clothes and jewelry. This was my androgynous reality, and being a "dyke" seemed more acceptable than being transgender.

I was not a cross-dresser or a drag queen, so, to me, it was better that I identify as same-gender-loving. Culturally, in such a relationship, one of y'all is "supposed" to be the man, anyway. So it was easy for them to accept me as a butch. I also accepted the labels and took on the behavior associated with them.

It was like a trial run of being a man in public—as if to say "Ha! The joke is on y'all because what you don't know is that I actually identify as a *man*!" This was as close to a man as I thought I could get. So, I would allow for the talk of damnation, the ridicule, and the verbal castration that I received from parishioners and leadership in the church. I did not want to walk away from my church or be shunned from it, so I acquiesced, allowing myself to sink deeper into dishonesty.

Living like a lesbian, instead of a man, never felt right. Of course, it wouldn't, right?! But, it was better for me to live a lie than to be shunned from the place that I loved so much—my church, "the" church, the Body of Christ.

How can a place that is supposed to be filled with love cause you to want to die? I was trained from childhood that suicide is a sin, and, if you commit it, that means your eternal resting place would be in hell. You would never see heaven because you took God's power and place by taking a life God created—even if the life was your own.

I did want to die, but I did not want to kill myself. In fact, I became so miserable that I did not care if I lived or I died. I was conflicted but not so much about my identity. I was conflicted about the love of God and why I could not see it in the eyes of others who called themselves believers. Love makes me want to be honest. Love makes me want to live in integrity. Love is what makes me tell the truth, even if my truth hurts you.

How could I be loved when I was being judged so harshly? How could I show up at a church service, still living a lie so deep? I was focusing on the "eyes" of others and what I showed them—what they saw. Instead, I needed to be focused on what *God* saw when God looked at me.

I have always loved to sing. I never claimed to be Grammy-level good, but singing to the glory of God was always what I wanted to do. Finding a place that was church-centered that would allow me to participate was life-changing for me. I joined a well-known gospel choir. I thought I found a place that I could call home. I was among people who were like me—or so I assumed.

What I did not know was that there were still stipulations for membership. Everything has a cost. I could hang out, travel, and party with my family, but only as long as I kept quiet about who I really was.

Yet, once I came into my true self, I was excited to share the good news! Right around the corner from joy, disappointment was waiting. I soon found out that though I was in the midst of people who were "like" me, I still could not be free to be me!

I always believed that singing in this choir, doing what I loved, would be the only place that I could be honest about being transgender. When I revealed my truth, I was shunned, talked about, and made to feel like an outsider among my peers—the saints of God! I soon found out that I was not loved the way I thought I was. I certainly was not being loved the way that I loved them. I was resented for coming out as transgender, as my full self. I just wanted to be free, so they could also be free.

Meanwhile, I found the love of God in a whole new way once I told the truth. I wanted to share that story and be a witness to the unconditional love of God! The rejection that I experienced during my transition made me pray harder. I learned to stand on the Word of God and to love those who despised me.

In fact, I was put in a position to demonstrate a love *for* them that I was no longer receiving *from* them. I would have to question if I ever actually received their love in the first place.

I learned that when you are free, you want others to be free. Love does not want anyone to be in pain. I had to un-learn and re-teach myself the true nature of God. Living in my truth illuminated some of the teaching of my former years as false.

Love does not hurt. Love does not put you in spaces that are not safe. Love is an action word. Love is when I am able to show that I care for a person, when we share mutual trust, respect, and compromise for one another. This is how we say we love one another, by sharing love.

Because of this re-learning season, I now know what love looks like for me. It has not been an easy journey. However, it has allowed me to *be*, to *be* Ryan Amir Harris, to be truthful and to walk in integrity. It has allowed me to walk as Christ walked, to love as Christ loved, to exist as Christ existed. Thank God, I am free!

I did go to that vigil for Leelah. I met those kids. I was even able to accompany one of them and his mother all the way through his transition. We are family to this day. Praise God that neither one of us has to be alone any more! Thank you, Leelah, for speaking your truth. We will go and do likewise (Luke 10:37).

Notes

Deacon Ryan Amir Harris (pronouns he/him) is a native of Cincinnati, Ohio, and a trans man of color. He is a deacon in his church, a father, and an uncle. He is a retired corrections officer and a community activist who enjoys family, friends, and traveling. He is happiest when he is serving the community.

Leelah Alcorn died by suicide on December 28, 2014. Her suicide note asked that all of her belongings be donated to transgender advocacy and requested that there be more education about gender identity in schools. Please call Trans Lifeline (877-565-8860) if you need help. The Trevor Project also offers support by phone, text, and online chat.

Transgender celebrity Laverne Cox popularized the term "possibility model" in 2014. Speaking on the ABC show *Katie* (hosted by Katie Couric), Cox clarified that she was not so arrogant as to want to be a "role model" that others should imitate, but that she does want to demonstrate that it is possible to live your dreams.

Suggested scripture

1 John 4—God Is Love

Matthew 5:44—Love Your Enemies

Luke 10:37—Go and Do Likewise

For further reflection

What does love look like to you? How has such a love shaped you?

Have you ever struggled with Christians who do not seem to be acting Christ-like? How have you coped with those situations?

What challenges in your life have helped you to own *your* truth?

In the Beginning

By Mycroft Masada

> *In the beginning, when God made heaven and earth, the world that we know had not yet come into being. There was nothing at all anywhere except a great emptiness and a living spirit which was God, moving as a mighty wind moves over dark waters.*

The Doubleday Illustrated Children's Bible, page 13

In the 1940's, my Aunt June was born. After college, she became an Episcopal nun, leaving Boston for New York. She left the order but remained an Episcopalian, moved to the Southwest, and met and married my Uncle John; they worked and lived on the Navajo reservation.

In 1976, I was born and assigned female, and my mother named me June after her younger sister (and our birth month); June nicknamed me June-ior (a play on Junior).

Aunt June never returned to Boston; we visited her and Uncle John several times during my childhood and youth and exchanged mail and calls. Through her gifts of many kinds, June helped me begin to understand myself as a person of faith, a faith leader, a social justice advocate, a reader, a writer, and an artist. She taught me that the Native people of our country were a vital part of the present and future, not just the past—a lesson I did not learn in my generally good public schools or elsewhere in my childhood, despite a strong Native community in Boston, Massachusetts, and New England. June connected us to the current voices of Native people, especially through their artwork. This extraordinary woman, and couple, living and working near Window Rock, Arizona, opened many windows for me.

As a child, I knew that my family was Jewish on my father's side and Christian on my mother's, but our practices were cultural and secular, apart from any faith community, and there was little time or energy for spiritual guidance at home. However, there was also very little faith-based or other bigotry, and my brother and I were encouraged to accept friends' invitations to their faith communities.

In 1983, when I was seven, Doubleday published *The Doubleday Illustrated Children's Bible* by Sandol Stoddard, with paintings by Tony Chen.

Aunt June sent me a copy of the Deluxe Edition as a gift.

It was the first Bible I had encountered, and one of the fanciest books I had ever seen. It lived in a gift box, white cardboard covered in cream-colored paper, with a cropped version of the illustration from its "Noah and the Flood" story. Noah in a brilliant pink robe and dramatic pose, and another person in blue, were directing pairs of animals into the Ark: dromedaries, bears, oryx, giraffes, cows, horses, painted dogs, flamingos, rhinos, zebras, ibex! They were joined by zebu, lions, Bactrian camels, ostriches, African and Asian elephants, monkeys and more!

The Book was bound in natural-looking cream-colored linen—much like the robes my Jewish ancestors, including Jesus, had worn, and the *tallitot* (prayer shawls) we wear now—with the title in big, shiny gold block letters. It had a purple satin ribbon as a bookmark, and even then I knew that was the color of royalty—and my favorite color.

It had bright blue endpapers and flyleaves, a color reflected in the waters, skies, garments, and other aspects of the illustrations. The first page had lines for writing who the Bible was "To" and "From" below an illustration of a lamb, both within a border of morning glories—and only the flowers were colored, each in that beautiful blue.

There were 138 beautiful, colorful, intense watercolors! I have remembered most of them to this day—some more than others:

Jacob Meets an Angel—their wrestling so full of drama and motion and emotion, and so much like a dance, with the angel looking rather non-binary to me, even at first sight.

Moses—being found by Pharaoh's daughter and her handmaidens, with lotus and papyrus growing in the foreground and an Egyptian boat full of busy people in the back.

Crossing the Sea—Pharoah and his troops about to be consumed by the waves, their fear so apparent that I felt for them, and how much more so for their horses.

The Cloud and the Fire—Miriam, rightly called Prophetess in the text, and four other women, in several bright colors of headscarves, tops, and skirts, looking about to levitate as they celebrate.

The Witch of Endor—the ghost of Samuel, in his glowing white cloak, with his scarily stony face and foot! The Witch, complete with wand, looking quite terrified by her success! King Saul, on his knees, reaching desperately for the prophet. All under a blue crescent moon in an inky sky above a dark landscape.

David the King—"dancing for God," being "a fool for God," as he leads a festive procession.

The Story of Jonah—about to be swallowed up by the great fish, as the sailors watch and gesture from the storm-rocked boat.

Belshazzar's Feast—recoiling in horror from the Hebrew-fonted words on his wall: "MENE, / MENE, / TEKEL, UP- / HARSIN" (Do disembodied hands use hyphens?).

Lazarus Raised—bandaged like a mummy, in a sand-colored robe! As Jesus and two women reach toward him, while a man appears to reach for Jesus, and two others roll the tombstone away.

The Garden of Gethsemane—three guards with torches and drawn swords, just a few inches away from Judas's back, whose front is even closer to Jesus, their faces almost touching, their beards appearing intertwined.

Birthday of the Church—three men and two women on their knees praying, a tongue of flame above each head.

Revelation—the Four Horsemen of the Apocalypse! Conquest and Victor, War, Famine, and Plague (looking something like the ghost of Samuel), floating in a sunset sky.

These are the pictures I have pictured every time I've encountered these stories since:

When I studied Ancient Egypt in school, at home, and beyond.

When I was at *shul* (synagogue), and we wrestled with the drowning of the Egyptians each year.

When I was taught Debbie Friedman's Miriam's Song. "And the women dancing with their timbrels / Followed Miriam as she sang her song! / Sing a song to the One whom we've exalted / Miriam and the women danced and danced the whole night long…"

When I met Jews who were against witches, and I challenged them.

When we studied the Book of Jonah each Yom Kippur.

53

When I went to Pentecost services, and found them to be flaming, festive birthday celebrations.

In addition to its diversity of landscapes, plants, creatures, and structures, this Book held some diversity of people and ideas, as well—a good-faith 1980's effort at both historical accuracy and modernization was begun, though not completed. There was the start of some sex, gender, and sexuality diversity. There were people of several races, including a few Black people that were not biblical characters; there was still far too much whiteness. The only visibly disabled people were those Jesus healed, and there did not seem to be any fat people; there was not much other body diversity. There was some spiritual diversity, though it was not presented in a very positive light.

There were also many of the challenging conflicts that have always been in grown-up Bibles, not to mention in our world—creation and distruction, climate change and in/justice, emigration and immigration and other migration, war and peace, slavery and freedom, misogyny and feminism, social injustice and justice, liberation and oppression, love and hate and indifference. Life and death—and life again! And, it was not short on stories about the economy, education, violence, or healthcare!

Too, it introduced me to some of my LGBTQ+ ancestors:

Joseph—three of his adult brothers casting the boy into a well, while two more drag his coat of many colors, painted in bright primary-colored stripes, off his shoulder and out of his hand.

Ruth and Naomi—Ruth standing and embracing Naomi as she sits. "Do not ask me again, I pray you, to leave your side or turn from your company. For wherever you go, there will I go also; and wherever you dwell, that shall be my home. Your people shall be my people; and your God shall be my God. Wherever you die, there I will die and be buried. May I suffer the wrath of the Lord if I part from you, even in death!" (from Ruth 1-16–17).

David and Jonathan—illustrated as if to deemphasize their relationship, and yet the text still said "The warriors loved David, and the king's son Jonathan came to love the young hero as if their two souls were one," and "'Go in peace,' said Jonathan, also in tears. 'God will be witness of our love for one another, now and forever!'" In fact, it was these partners who first gave me my second name. "Again the two friends parted, and David took his band of men to the stronghold of Engedi, a mountain fortress that was later known as Masada."

The Song of Solomon—framed by text and artwork as a "celebration of the love of man and woman," but even to my childish eyes clearly more complex.

Esther—courageously coming out to her king on his throne. "Spare my people, and give me my own life, for I am also a Jew!"

Daniel, though without his Ashpenaz.

The Roman centurion and his servant.

The high-ranking Ethiopian official.

None of the supposedly anti-LGBTQ bits of the Bible are included in the Book—and as I eventually learned, neither the Torah nor the Bible are actually anti-LGBTQ+. In my Bible's story, the Destruction of Sodom and Gomorrah occurs because they have broken "God's sacred laws of hospitality"—and, in the illustration, the looks on Lot's and his daughters' faces are heartbroken and heartbreaking, as behind them burns the ruins of their home, and there stands the statue of salt that was his wife and their mother.

The second Bible I encountered was my mother's. She had a small, personal edition, bound in white leather, with all edge gilt. June and I think it may have belonged to their mother. I think it was the only other Bible we had in our home. Mum did not speak about it often, but she did give me a sense of its use and potential for oppression and liberation, of women and others.

As the 1990's began, and I entered high school, I began to identify and express myself as a trans and queer person, and to use the name Mycroft more—though June remained a vital part of me in every sense. At the turn of the century, my mother passed away, due to the complications of her alcoholism; may her memory be a blessing, as we say in Judaism. My brother had come to identify as a Christian, and I gave him Mum's Bible. I began to identify as a Jew and a Jewscopalian. Uncle John passed away; may his memory be a blessing as well. I met, married, and adopted a dogter with a wonderful, fat, queer, cis, mas(s)culine-presenting woman. My spouse Julia is agnostic, raised in the United Methodist Church, and her spiritual journey and practice include my traditions and others.

For me, being interfaith and intergender has always been intertwined. I am a child of an interfaith family who is an interfaith person in an interfaith marriage. I am a child of Jews who is a Jew, but not only a

Jew; a niecephew of an Episcopalian who is a different kind of Episcopalian; and more so a Jewscopalian. A trans mentor of mine used to ask if, since we used "intersex" when talking about the spectrum between male and female, we might use "intergender" to talk about the space between man and woman, and I still think that is a good question. I am female, but in a different sense than cis or trans women. I have tried living in a few genders and sexualities, and I now live as a non-binary trans person who is also queer. I am both/neither/other than a woman or man, and I am attracted to women, men, and others. I usually use the pronouns they/them/theirs, she/her/hers, and zie/hir/hirs.

Aunt June has continued to love, accept, support, encourage, and celebrate me and my family, much as always. She asked if she could still call me June-ior, and I gladly said yes.

After I left my parents' house as a young adult, many of my childhood books and toys went missing, including my Bible. I thought about, referenced, and missed it often. I added a menorah to my collection because it reflected one of my favorite illustrations—two of the twelve Israelite spies bear a bunch of grapes, almost as big as they are, past a dark tree with bright fruit, while figs and pomegranates bloom and grow in the foreground. A few of my Bible's illustrations included pomegranates, which became one of my favorite Jewish symbols and foods. I have included this connection each time I have presented my annual "Mycroft's Menorah Mishigas" show on social media.

A couple of years ago, I bought a copy of my Children's Bible on eBay. I greeted it like an old friend, a gift from an old friend—from my divinely inspired writer ancestors, from God. Our reunion brought new meaning to yet another of its stories—A Book Is Found (adapted from 2 Kings 22:1–10 and 2 Chronicles 34)!

I am still learning about Sandol Stoddard and her team. She died in 2018, and her primary obituary says that, in addition to being a pioneer in the hospice movement and an environmental justice advocate, "she was active in Marin County education issues and an outspoken supporter of equal rights for women, minorities, and the LGBT community." And while I couldn't recommend this Bible for even the most mature children, it could work well for youth, with good guidance. I believe everyone should be introduced to the Torah, Bible, Qur'an and other scriptures as early as possible. However, like most "children's" Bibles, this one's text and illustrations need a great quantity and quality of context and conversation from adults.

Last year, I was asked to write a piece for the book you are reading. I was already working on a piece about my Children's Bible. It seemed *bashert* (meant to be), for this book to become the first home of my story of my first Book.

Someday, Aunt June will pass on to the next life. Probably many years after, I will join her. Our bodies and our Bibles will remain behind. Maybe, I will pass my Children's Bible on to someone else before I pass. Maybe I will let go and let God. June and I will become ashes. Our Books will become dust. And, God willing, their Words and ours will continue to do good work in this world.

What would happen now to all the hopes and dreams of Abraham's descendants, the people who looked to the book of Law and the holy Temple as the central power in their daily life? What would happen to those who still waited faithfully for the House of David to bring them a Messiah, a kingdom, and peace on earth?

The Doubleday Illustrated Children's Bible, page 222

Notes

Mycroft Masada is a nonbinary trans and queer faith leader with almost 30 years of experience. A TransEpiscopal Steering Committee member and former Congregation Am Tikva board member, Mycroft is particularly called to pursue LGBTQ+ and fat justice, as an advocate, organizer, consultant, educator, trainer, writer, and artist. A Bostonian until 2014, they live in Gaithersburg, Maryland, with their spouse Julia McCrossin and dogter Ursula.

The opening and closing quotes here are also the opening and closing words of the "Old Testament" in the *The Doubleday Illustrated Children's Bible* (1983), by Sandol Stoddard, with paintings by Tony Chen.

"Miriam's Song" by Debbie Friedman appeared on her *And You Shall Be a Blessing* album (1988).

Suggested scripture

Ruth 1—Ruth and Naomi

I Samuel 18:1, 19:1–7, 20, and II Samuel 1:26—Jonathon and David

Luke 7:1–10 and Matthew 8:5–13—Roman Centurion and His Servant

For further reflection

How have relationships in your family of origin influenced your understanding of Christian faith?

What memories do you have of childhood religious formation? How has your understanding of those early teachings shifted over time?

Masada reads this gift from a Christian family member, in part, through the experiences they have had with Jewish family members. Do the traditions and heirlooms you have inherited tell a simple story—or a story with layers and complexity?

Songs of Struggle, Songs of Resilience

By Debra J. Hopkins

One of my favorite hymns is "Sweet Hour of Prayer." It captures some of the complexity of being a Black, transgender woman:

Sweet hour of prayer
Sweet hour of prayer
That calls me from a world of care
And bids me at my Father's throne
Make all my wants and wishes known.
In seasons of distress and grief
My soul has often found relief
And oft escaped the tempter's snare
By Thy return, sweet hour of prayer.

Transgender and gender nonconforming people often face discrimination in our day-to-day lives. That includes discrimination and mistreatment when accessing public accommodations, obtaining housing, or medical care, and even while seeking employment. These challenges and their consequences (for example, poverty or trauma) are some of the struggles that prevent us from thriving.

Meanwhile, resilience is the quality of being able to adapt to stressful life changes. It is our "bounce back" from hardship. Resilience is also a part of life for transgender and gender nonconforming people. Sometimes, it is easy to overemphasize the struggles and forget to be inspired by the insight, wisdom, and discernment that accompany our survival.

Songs of struggle. Songs of resilience. Both of these songs are a part of my life as a 63-year-old Black, transgender woman living in North Carolina.

Some years back, in 2007, I was arrested and held overnight. It turned out to be a bizarre case of mistaken identity, but even one night in jail can be extremely dangerous for a transgender woman like myself. The police mistreated me. I was beaten and then raped by the other inmates.

As a Christian pastor, I always look to scripture to guide me. Holding on to Bible verses helps me stay faithful and encouraged during

Debra J. Hopkins

times of trial:

> *We are hard pressed on every side, but not crushed;*
> *perplexed, but not in despair;*
> *persecuted, but not abandoned;*
> *struck down, but not destroyed.*

2 Corinthians 4:8–9 NIV

I was transferred from the jail to a hospital for treatment afterwards. While I was waiting in the hallway of the emergency room, a doctor approached me and told me to strip off my clothes. Naturally, I refused. The doctor opened the door to an exam room and instructed me to go inside. However, the doctor remained in the hallway, refusing to enter the room. He ordered x-rays for me from the hallway.

Later, he returned to give me the results. I had a broken nose and a badly sprained neck. Still standing in the doorway, never having gotten close enough to examine me, he reported that there was no physical sign of my having been raped. He sent someone in to give me a neck brace and walked away, never to be seen again.

Resilience does not mean avoiding trouble. It means finding enough strength to cope with what comes our way. Of course, discrimination and violence should not be considered blessings. Yet, as a Christian, I believe that God does not count it robbery to dwell among us, even in the midst of our messiest human dilemmas. My struggles have helped me to feel God's presence more deeply.

> *The Lord makes firm the steps*
> *of the one who delights in him;*
> *though he may stumble, he will not fall,*
> *for the Lord upholds him with his hand.*

Psalm 37:23–24 NIV

My ordeal did not end with the doctor that night. Later, two police officers walked into my room where I was still waiting, dressed in a skirt and blouse. Naturally, fear began to rise up in me because of the abuse I had received from other officers back at the jail earlier that same day.

These officers looked at me with a smirk on their faces and said in unison: "How can we help you, sir?"

I froze for a moment as the fear in me swelled. In addition to the physical pain I was enduring as a result of the beating and rape, I was now terrified about what would happen next. I gathered myself and, finally, I screamed for them to leave at the top of my voice, "Get OUT!"

The Bible contains many admonitions to press on (Philippians 3:13–15), overcome hardship and temptation (Romans 12:21), and persevere in the face of trials (James 1:12). Of course, that is easier said than done when it seems that even those sent to "help" or "protect" you turn against you.

That night in 2007, I went home and attempted to take my life. Glory to God I survived!

In time, I became connected to many LGBTQ activists and leaders locally and around the country. My resilience allowed me to be present both to receive and eventually to give a lot of support. Now, I serve as the executive director of a small homeless shelter serving adults of transgender experience in the Greater Charlotte area.

However, that night in jail and in the hospital still haunts me. For years, I drove over three hours to find medical care because I feared having the same experience again with local doctors. To this day, I still fear reaching out to the police for help because of how they handled me on that particular night.

The need for this kind of resilience is pervasive, especially for transgender youth and women of color. My story is just one example of how so many transgender women of color adaptively respond to the discrimination and prejudice we encounter in the world.

The Bible also gives us numerous examples of people who suffered greatly but continued to follow God's plan for their lives. After the apostle Paul had his life-altering encounter with Jesus (Acts 9) and was transformed from a religious Pharisee to a radical Christian, many were not happy with his message. He was criticized, jailed, beaten, stoned, and nearly killed many times (2 Corinthians 11:24–27).

In Lystra in Asia Minor, he was stoned, dragged out of town, and left for dead. However, when his enemies left, Paul got up and went back into the city (Acts 14:19–20). His missionary endeavors continued unabated. Godly resilience also enables us as trans people to be undeterred from our mission, regardless of the opposition.

> *Trust in the LORD with all your heart,*
> *and lean not on your own understanding.*
> *In all your ways acknowledge him,*
> *and he shall direct your paths.*

Proverbs 3:5–6 NKJV

Like Paul and so many other saints, I choose to trust in the Lord, even in the midst of a culture that considers me (and others like me) a dangerous "other." I walk with my head held high, confident in God's grace, rather than relying only on my own understanding. I give thanks that I can also help others to persevere, despite whatever losses we endure.

Research about victimization among sexual minority youth and trans women of color has focused on documenting the prevalence of discrimination and sometimes violence against us. Yet, little has been written in formal literature exploring our risk and our resilience in terms of the social context in which we struggle. We are not just random victims. We are also survivors. We are creative. We are resourceful. We have to be, as we navigate systems that want to erase us at every turn.

My story is only one among many told by brave and courageous individuals who have made a commitment to fighting against injustice. When people refuse to give up on themselves and the world, even after severe or persistent misfortune, it is not always beautiful. It is not always harmonious or elegant. On some days, it may be all we can do to yell something as unceremonious as, "Get OUT!"

Yet, screaming and crying for my life that night was also a song of struggle. Even our wailing and our raging can be songs of resilience as we reach for a better day. I work every day to rise above a constant stream of bigotry, discrimination, and hate to continue on as a voice for change. The journey is not easy, but we are never alone.

Sweet hour of prayer
Sweet hour of prayer
Thy wings shall my petition bear
to Him whose truth and faithfulness
engage the waiting soul to bless.
And since he bids me seek his face,
believe his word, and trust his grace,
I'll cast on him my every care,
and wait for thee, sweet hour of prayer!

Notes

The Reverend Debra Hopkins is a nondenominational minister and founding executive director of There's Still Hope, a nonprofit organization serving transgender adults who are experiencing homelessness in the Greater Charlotte, North Carolina area. Hopkins is the proud parent of three adult children, eight beautiful grandchildren, and the author of three books. You can read more about her life in her memoir, titled *Not Until You Have Walked in My Shoes A Journey of Discovery & the Spirit of the Human Heart*, forthcoming in 2020 and available from Amazon.

The words to "Sweet Hour of Prayer" were written by William W.

Walford (1772-1850).

Suggested scripture

2 Corinthians 4—Renewal and Resistance

Psalm 37—Song of Resistance

Proverbs 3—Wisdom as Fortification

For further reflection

Have you ever been faced with challenges in your life that have driven you to despair?

Where do you find hope, or what do you cling to in times of struggle?

How does your life weave together songs of struggle and songs of resilience? Is one louder or more prominent than the other?

The Ethiopian Eunuch—and Me

By Mir Plemmons

As they went along the road they came to some water;
and the eunuch said, "Look! Water!
What prevents me from being baptized?"

And Philip said, "If you believe with all your heart, you may."

And he answered and said,
"I believe that Jesus Christ is the Son of God."

And he ordered the chariot to stop;
and they both went down into the water,
Philip as well as the eunuch, and he baptized him.

Acts 8:36-38 NASB

Most of the church says "the Ethiopian eunuch" the way we say "the Seattle Seahawks," with no more thought given to what a eunuch is than we think about what a seahawk is. Most of the church knows his story, but very few know mine. When I think "Ethiopian eunuch," I fully hear both words.

While I am not exactly a "eunuch" in terms of time and culture, I very much resonate with his circumstance. The current phrase for someone like me is coercively assigned female at birth and intersex. I was modified to fit a script—and it is always easier to cut something inconvenient off than fix it or see what happens. So, I was raised female—and then I attended a fundamentalist church in my teens. I tried hard to conform, comply, conceal (even from myself!) the scarred truth in my genitals. Reading this Acts 8 story is part of what finally made me whole.

My mental image of the "Ethiopian eunuch" story is well-worn, like stairs that I have walked many times, touching their familiar strength as they lift me up. Most gentiles use his story to speak of their right to baptism and membership in our holy priesthood of believers. I do, too—and seeing all of him means that the true (inclusive) Christian faith is clear right from the start of our tradition.

This eunuch was in violation of Deuteronomy 23:1. A eunuch had no official right to go up to Jerusalem to worship. He literally could not be in the assembly. But, here he was, reading scripture—on lunch break, I guess—coming back from presenting as a cismale in the gentile Court of the Temple.

We all know the phrase in American English slang for that: It took balls for this guy without balls to pretend he had balls. He did what he had to do in order to worship his God, regardless of what others might say or do—daring to chase his God even at the risk of being caught. It might even have felt as though his balls were in a vise—to make that choice and to follow through with it, despite what happened to him in his youth. Now, returning home victorious, there he was sitting in the back of his chariot, reading scripture. I can identify, almost completely, with a guy like that!

My struggles increased when puberty hit (twice). First, there was resentment (one set of hormones) and then confusion (when the second, but preferable, set of hormones finally kicked in). As a teen I was baptised with others, in the same weighted white robes regardless of gender, going down to the heated indoor pool, held, dunked, raised with water and tears streaming down our faces and the words of baptism echoing over our heads. My talks with God were only about gender when I was complaining—and even there, it was not about me. It was about what others were demanding of me.

I started having to conceal even more masculinization while being denied the things I felt called to because I was considered "a girl." For example, I coached the other guys to win preaching competitions I was not eligible to enter because of the way they saw me. Like any teen, I struggled with what I wished for versus how I saw myself. I struggled and shouted at the sky and failed to fit into any mold we tried. It got worse as I hit my late teens and started shaving. There I was, the one they thought would be the next great Christian apologist (explainer) despite "being a girl." The pressure and the conflict were too much for me to cope with. I went to college—and left the church.

That was not me, either, though. I learned that I could not leave God. I kept struggling with God, wounded like Jacob (just a bit more intimately than in the hip). I desperately wanted and needed an answer— some way to be strong in all of my truth and to fulfill my calling. One day, there he was, this Ethiopian eunuch, right there in the same book that, though I loved it, was being used to limit my options.

I could not find rest in the Bible, but I clung to it until from this same book leaped this eunuch, powerful and strong and politically savvy. He was calmly claiming his place in Jerusalem's Temple to worship. How I envied him! How I wished I was him! People would say "the Ethiopian

Eunuch" like it was one word. Not to me. He was so much more than just the foreigner, the gentile.

As I read and reread, I learned that he was a man whose scarred truth made him the powerful leader he was. I learned the incredibly subversive truth that this first story of a non-Jewish convert baptised on the roadside was a cut man—like myself. This was a radical welcome in the newborn church. Philip was told to leave a very successful preaching project to take a remote road, solely to find this *eunuch*—a eunuch strong enough in his faith and sense of self to defy the entire establishment to take his place in the Temple, yet humble enough to welcome this traveling Galilean preacher who ran up to his chariot asking questions.

The Ethiopian eunuch invited Philip aboard his chariot. How powerful is it that he continued his own journey? He was clear in his purpose in every way. He invited Philip to come along for the ride and teach him. That was exactly why Philip was there, so he said yes. This is what God does for each of us!

We cannot know how long they traveled with Philip as the eunuch's guest and teacher before they saw a river or spring near the road. Perhaps the voice of the water called to this humble, gutsy, determined eunuch leader. He looked at Philip and called for a demonstration of radical grace and acceptance. Hey, here's water. And you. And me. And I believe. *So*, what is to keep me from getting baptized?!

Philip's response? Not a blessed thing. Let's do it.

That realization washed over me. My sense of self has repeatedly felt the sudden splash of revelation, the shock of the "a-ha" like a cold, refreshing splash of living water streaming down my face and through my awareness. I think I gained more from the Ethiopian eunuch's baptism than my own.

As a teen, I was dunked and claimed and told "I baptise you…". Yet, later, in another denomination, a Bishop put his hand on my forehead and told me to *remember your baptism*. In that moment, I remembered the shocking, water-and-light-filled invitation that had truly claimed me for God—so much more than the warm pool where they had claimed for God only the parts of "me" that they could accept. This overwhelming cleansing claimed *all* of me for God—as God does. These Truths embraced my own truths and filled them with God's light.

Afterwards, the Ethiopian eunuch's baptiser, Philip, vanished— much like (though more miraculously than) those folk who washed me with grace as I learned the depth of welcome that is truly our faith. Their work in us was complete, and each of us moved forward with the blessing of having worked together—with the joy of having shared God's deep, radical grace. Like the Ethiopian eunuch, I, too, have gone on my way into my ministry rejoicing in all that God has done for and with me.

This is the Good News, proclaimed to each one of us. Thanks be to God!

Notes

Mir Plemmons is a Franciscan Friar and Chaplain, in formation to regularize his priesthood in the Ecumenical Catholic Communion. He teaches students with special needs and lives with his wife almost far enough away from Seattle for comfort.

Actually, the Acts 8 traveler is not the only Ethiopian eunuch in the Christian Bible. Look up Jeremiah 38 for the story of Ebed Melech and see Chapter 15 in *OtherWise Christian: A Guidebook for Transgender Liberation* (2019) by Mx Chris Paige. Meanwhile, watch for *OtherWise Christian 3*, which is expected to be an anthology of further reflections on this powerful story of Philip and the Acts 8 traveler.

Suggested scripture

Acts 8:26–40—The Story of the Ethiopian Eunuch (see Chapter 15 of *OtherWise Christian*)

Deuteronomy 23:1 (also Leviticus 21:20)—Law about Crushed and Cut Genitalia (see Chapter 10 of *OtherWise Christian*)

Genesis 32:24–32—Jacob Wrestling God (or the Angel) and Getting His Hip Hurt

For further reflection

Have you ever been able to imagine that someone in the Bible might be like you? How does it feel to think about an OtherWise-gendered character as someone so pivotal?

How does it feel to read someone who is talking, even light-heartedly, about their own genitalia and that of a Bible character?

What are your own experiences with baptism(s)? Have you experienced baptism as a radical statement of inclusion?

Wrestling Like Jacob

By Victoria S. Kolakowski

Then the man said,
"Your name will no longer be Jacob, but Israel,
because you have struggled with God
and with humans and have overcome."

Genesis 32:28 NIV

There is power in a name.

Names are connected to our identity. When someone asks who you are, most people respond with their name. It is more than a label; it is something that has a deep connection to who we are.

Names have meanings. Most of us do not think about the literal meanings, but they exist, and I think that, at some level, they flavor us. I have heard people say on many occasions "So and So doesn't look like a Mary/Karen/Toby/whatever." I do not really know what that means, but somehow people have impressions about what someone with a particular name is like.

I remember encountering the Nobel Prize-winning physicist Dr. Eugene Wigner at a reception. He said to me, "Kolakowski... what does 'Kolakowski' mean?"

I said that it meant nothing.

"Oh, so you don't know then" was his reply. He was right: It has an actual, literal meaning, and I did not know it yet.

Most of us do not get to choose our own names. Our parents choose for us. Pop stars choose their names the most—Madonna, Elton John, Freddie Mercury, Lady Gaga, Childish Gambino, to name a few. Sometimes movie actors do. Writers may use a *nom de plume*—a pen name.

Some people dislike their name enough that they change it. Some use a middle name or a nickname. Others choose something totally new. Sometimes, the name change is informal, and other times it is legally binding. As a judge, one of the happiest groups of people that I see is when I cover the name-change calendar. Everyone is so thrilled to be officially recognized!

Names are important for trans people, for those reasons and others. Many trans people are offended to be addressed by the names they

69

were assigned by their parents, because it asserts an identity that did not fit. There is even a term for this. "Deadnaming" is when a name is used to describe a person who does not really exist in any meaningful way any more (if they ever did). Our birth names are (well-meaning) fictions that we typically put to rest as we claim a more authentic identity.

One of my favorite biblical passages is about a name change. Genesis 32:22–32 is commonly known as "Jacob Wrestling with the Angel." Jacob was a fascinating person. He started out life being the second born of two male twins. He and his brother Esau had one of the most serious sibling rivalries recorded in ancient history. Jacob is probably best known for tricking his father Isaac into giving Jacob his blessing by pretending to be Esau.

Jacob was the one tricked later on. He worked for seven years to marry his beloved Rachel, only to have her swapped out by his father-in-law, Laban, so that he married her older sister, Leah, instead. Jacob had to work seven more years to be able to marry Rachel. Jacob's ladder is also in Jacob's story, but more people know the term than the actual story.

Well, Jacob received a vision in a dream warning him to leave Laban and go home to Canaan. So, he left along with his flocks, children, wives, concubines, and servants. When he neared his old home, he sent a scout ahead. The scout reported that Esau was waiting with a few of his friends—with 400 warriors to be specific.

This was a terrifying moment for Jacob. He knew his moment of reckoning was literally on the horizon. He had done his brother wrong, and he was no match for Esau's army. So, Jacob sent everyone else ahead, hoping that Esau would spare them. Then, Jacob hunkered down for a long, dark, and terrifying night.

In the night, Jacob was visited by someone. The scriptures variously call it a man, an angel, and even God. They did what any normal people would do when meeting in the dark of night: They wrestled each other until daybreak. What?! That wasn't what I would have done, but okay!

They wrestled and wrestled, and Jacob would not release the stranger. As dawn approached, the mysterious stranger touched Jacob's hip, which became dislocated. And still, Jacob demanded a blessing. Apparently, Jacob was really into getting his blessings by any means necessary!

> So Jacob was left alone, and a man wrestled with him till daybreak.

> When the man saw that he could not overpower him,
> he touched the socket of Jacob's hip
> so that his hip was wrenched as he wrestled with the man.

> Then the man said, "Let me go, for it is daybreak."

But Jacob replied, "I will not let you go unless you bless me."

The man asked him, "What is your name?"

"Jacob," he answered.

Then the man said, "Your name will no longer be Jacob, but Israel, because you have struggled with God and with humans and have overcome."

Jacob said, "Please tell me your name."

But he replied, "Why do you ask my name?"

Then he blessed him there.

So Jacob called the place Peniel, saying, "It is because I saw God face to face, and yet my life was spared."

The sun rose above him as he passed Peniel, and he was limping because of his hip.

Genesis 32:24–31 NIV

The stranger never did identify himself, and Jacob had a limp, but Jacob got his blessing—and a new name.

Israel was not just any man or Bible character. He was *the* Israel, the father of the twelve tribes, after whom the modern nation is founded. And, *he* had a name change—one that he earned by wrestling in the dark while he was afraid for his life.

We frequently say that we wrestle with something—a decision, our fears, the future. We do not mean it literally, like Jacob's encounter here. But, that sense of challenging, of holding on, of not giving up, of demanding the blessing can be there for each of us.

I struggled a lot around my gender identity. I was afraid of rejection, not just by people but by God. I was worried that I would be rejecting who I was *supposed* to be. I knew that I felt that I was a girl, then a woman, but others did not see it the way that I did. For a long time, I did not think there was anything I could do about it. It sounded preposterous—and how could I convince anyone that this was me?

Once I discovered that there was something that I could do, there was the fear of what would come afterwards. People could reject me—and, eventually, many did. But, I also became convinced that God would be there with, alongside me. This was a big surprise for me.

When I was still a kid, I had this prayer card that said that if I prayed this particular prayer to this particular saint every single day for a year, my prayer would be answered. Every day, I prayed that I would wake up and be a girl. After a year, I kept praying, thinking that maybe I had missed a day. Maybe, if I kept going, it could still be answered.

I had no idea that my wish—which is what it really was—would be fulfilled (but not until I was an adult, and not the way that I expected). I got angry with God—furious, really.

I could not understand why I had been given someone else's perfect life. I had a loving family and good health. I was decent looking and smart. I had a whole bright future ahead of me, but it was a future as a guy. No pretty dresses. No handsome boyfriends (It never occurred to me that I would fall in love with a woman). Never giving birth. Never being a Mommy.

I knew, to my core, that I was not a "Michael." But who was I? What would I call myself—even if nobody else ever called me by my name? I immediately rejected Michele or Michelle. The idea of just running with a feminized version of a given name did not seem right for me. I wanted more distance than that. Nothing that began with an M would do.

Even so, my first thoughts went to "M" names. "Margaret" seemed like a good choice. I liked the name "Meg," partly because one of my favorite literary characters was Meg from *A Wrinkle in Time*. I could get that from Margaret, although I was worried that I would get stuck with people calling me "Peggy"—which I would not appreciate. I could have gone with Megan.

Instead, I went with "Victoria." It is a royal name. An entire age is named after Queen Victoria. It is a winning name.

It is a perfect name for a woman who knew that she would have to fight and win. My name was like my armor. It was a constant affirmation— a reminder never to let go. Although I did not know it at the time, this name said that I could wrestle with an angel—and that I would overcome.

I started to come out to some people close to me during my first year in college. I was 17 at the time, and I had a few close friends. They pretty much all accepted me—and several were Christian. I fell in love with a guy, who would later go on to seminary and marry a wonderful woman. They remain my friends. He saw me as a woman.

Something happened to me that year as I started having those conversations. I do not know exactly when. There was no "a-ha" moment of clarity, but something inside me shifted. I developed the firm belief that I would be myself, but that I could only prevail with God on my side. I needed that blessing, and something inside told me that it was coming. So, I held on tight.

There have been many dark moments—times of fear, times of rejection, times of immense loneliness. It was often hard to hold on. Eventually, I, too, limped away from the struggle—literally. After my gender confirmation surgery, I found that part of my left thigh was permanently numb. I assume that I was mispositioned during the day-long surgery.

Sometimes, I wish that my journey had been one where I did not need to be a Victoria. I wish that I could have been a Megan without so much struggle. But, my personal mantra is from the great movie, *Galaxy Quest*: "Never Give Up, Never Surrender!" My journey required that I be a Victoria. I was going to be one who wrestles and holds on.

The story of Jacob/Israel and Esau had a happy ending. When they met later in the light of day, they embraced. Esau got to meet his sisters-in-law, nieces, and nephews. It was a storybook finale.

I often wonder whether it would have been different if it were Jacob who met Esau instead of Israel. How might things have been different, if Jacob did not tarry in his fear. Were Jacob's fears unfounded? Was all of that wrestling for naught?

I like to think that the wrestling was part of what brought peace and healing to the situation. Something changed that allowed Jacob to face his brother as a different man. I believe that it is only through our wrestling with challenges that we become better equipped to handle life's scariest moments. As for me, I never intend to stop holding on until my blessing is complete.

Notes

The Reverend Victoria S. Kolakowski (she/her) received her M.Div. from the Pacific School of Religion in 1998. She was the first person to have a transgender-positive article published in an academic religious journal in 1997. She was ordained in the Metropolitan Community Church as the first person to start and complete the ordination process as an openly transgender person. She served as clergy at several churches, and on the board of the California Council of Churches. She retired from ministry when she became a judge in Alameda County, California, in 2011.

There is much to be said about the lineage of Abraham, Isaac, Jacob, and Joseph in terms of gender. Mx Chris Paige summarizes some of these insights in *OtherWise Christian: A Guidebook for Transgender Liberation*, but we also strongly recommend Joy Ladin's *Soul of a Stranger: Reading God and Torah from a Transgender Perspective*.

Suggested scripture

Genesis 32:22–32—Jacob and the Angel

Hosea 12:2–6—Jacob and the Angel, in Hindsight

Psalm 22—My God, My God, Why Have You Forsaken Me?

For further reflection

What does your name mean to you? Have you ever chosen a name for yourself?

Have you ever been angry with God? What were you taught growing up (for instance, by religion, culture, or family) about anger?

Have you ever tried to convince someone of who you are when there is no documentation or credential to be shown? Are there times when you have felt the need to be stubborn or assertive in order to be recognized? From what sources of strength did you draw for that struggle?

Discipleship

By RJ Robles

*Jesus went up on a mountainside
and called to him those he wanted,
and they came to him.*

Mark 3:13 NIV

My mama, Teresa Robles Rodriguez Soto, was the one who showed me how to read the Bible when I was younger and growing up in a Latino church of the Puerto Rican diaspora. My maternal Tio, Jorge Rodriguez, was the person who taught me about the Orishas as a practicing Santero when I would go on family vacations to visit him in the Bronx of New York City. With support from my *familia* really early on, I sought out both my ancestral practices of faith and began the process of unlearning Christian supremacy.

When I first picked up the Bible for myself early on in my transgender journey, I quickly fell in love with the Gospel of Mark. Believed to be the earliest Gospel text, the story in Mark tells us about the Son of God coming into our world, shaking things up, and challenging our perceptions about what God is truly like. In the midst of this Holy Disruption, God invites us to change the things we think are important. As we shift and adjust, God also changes our circumstances, heals our bodies and our traumas, and fixes the pressing needs of our relationships with our friends, chosen family, lovers, and intimate partners. The fundamental way Jesus changes us, is by giving each of us a new name. By doing that, he shapes both the identity and the destiny of our lives.

In the story of Mark, Chapter 3, we see Jesus re-naming people. He is at the height of his ministry. Huge crowds—people from a hundred miles away—have come on foot at the news of this miraculous healer. At this great point of being known, Jesus goes away to the mountain—and he starts re-naming his disciples. Scripture says he appointed twelve, designating them (naming them) disciples. And then, he also gave new names to some of the disciples: To Simon he gave the name Peter ("Rock"), to James and John, he gave the name Boanerges ("Sons of Thunder"). What does this name change mean? Why was it important?

He appointed twelve that they might be with him
and that he might send them out to preach
and to have authority to drive out demons.

Mark 3:14–15 NIV

The church I belonged to growing up was a very conservative Latino congregation in Humboldt Park, Chicago. That was where I first encountered the message that "homosexuality and being transgender is a sinful lifestyle." When I was a teen, a pastor was praying for me. When he said my birth name, at just that moment, I heard God whisper to me, "You are my disciple, and I have called you RJ."

It was the beginning of my gender transition. While I would eventually leave the church, the name Jesus gave to me and my calling to Gospel ministry never left me.

The primary way Jesus works—the primary way he changes people—is by giving them a new name. By new name, I also mean a new identity. I mean that he changes the trajectory of your life entirely. He worked that way with the twelve disciples, and he works that way in the lives of all of his people.

Jesus gives each of us a new name. Jesus grows us into our new names. Jesus guarantees us glory, under our new names.

Jesus called the twelve disciples to him, and he gave each of them a new identity. They became the new Israel. They became the church. This was the foundation of the new religious movement that would eventually be called Christianity: the naming of the twelve disciples.

These are the twelve he appointed:
Simon (to whom he gave the name Peter),
James son of Zebedee and his brother John
(to them he gave the name Boanerges, which means "sons of thunder"),
Andrew, Philip, Bartholomew,
Matthew, Thomas, James son of Alphaeus,
Thaddaeus, Simon the Zealot
and Judas Iscariot, who betrayed him.

Mark 3:16–19 NIV

Let's think for a moment how incredible this is—how incredible it is that I have heard God's sweet, sweet whisper, "You are now my disciple, and you shall be known as RJ." I am so grateful for that moment. From that point on, I knew that my new identity was RJ.

76

This is also what Jesus has given to you, if he has called you. He has given you a new name and a new identity, too. He knows you, inside and out. The name that Jesus gives is a name that is solid and dependable.

What is your new name? Here is one: "disciple." Jesus calls you his "sheep" (John 10). His "friends" (John 15). His "siblings" and his "children" (Hebrews 2). His "kings" and "priests" (Revelation 1). Every one of these names brings with it a new identity that endures no matter what your experiences in life. When Jesus calls, he gives you a new name. My new name is RJ; what is yours?

I searched and searched for a home church that would honor my transness and my radical Brownness, but I did not find what I was looking for. Still, I felt this pull on my heart: the presence of the Holy Spirit, Yemaja, and my trans ancestors guiding me, pouring into me.

I had to deconstruct and rebuild my faith as my own. This involved a deep process of decolonization including a formal dive into Black and Brown queer and trans academic scholarship. I majored in Gender & Women's Studies at a public urban university in Chicago, Illinois, which provided me the intersectional analysis and framework that I had been struggling for years to name.

It was also there under the guidance of Black feminists, queer Chicanas, and trans Latinas that I learned to rely more heavily on my spirituality and faith. I found out about the role of liberation theology in the church and surrounded myself with queer and transgender Christian theological books. I met warriors and movement leaders, as well as other Black and Brown Indigenous LGBTQ faith leaders.

As I continued to engage in community organizing as a Brown, trans, non-binary person, I was also able to live more fully into RJ, disciple of Christ. I am now a community organizer, movement chaplain, trans theologian, queer scholar of color, and minister in the Christian Church (Disciples of Christ).

There's an outcast in everybody's life and I am her...

It's a hell of a world that we're living in James: a sin is a sin.
Don't look at me immediately, and
whisper behind my back thinking I'm naïve,
it's my southern hospitality,
tolerates more BS than even I can believe...

Don't care too much what other people say,
I get along swell by my goddamn self,
never asked for no one's philosophy,
it's obvious I'm proud of me.

There's an outcast in everybody's life and I am her...

Excerpts from "I Am Her" by Shea Diamond

"I Am Her" is a song written by a Black, transgender, soul singer, who found her voice in a men's prison. Shea Diamond says she wrote this song "to express all [her] feelings about the church, the rejection [I received] from the church, [and] how nobody wanted to accept me for being [myself]."

Ms. Diamond was put into isolation while she was incarcerated. She explains, "Being trans, they wanted to punish me extra—they wanted to [deprive] me of yard or telephone privileges just for being me."

So she spent a lot of time by herself, but the people whose cells were near her would hear the song and love it. These were mainly "straight men, who didn't identify as being allies or anything else, but they liked the song."

She explains, the song "talks about how, at the end of the day, I was by myself and I was all right by myself."

It is a shame when the church does not offer sanctuary. It is a shame that prisoners and convicts sometimes express more appreciation than church folk, but we can be ourselves fully, regardless of what people think or say—and Jesus will help us.

Growing into our new identities requires community. As trans folk, we constantly seek out community, and we build our own communities when others reject us. These communities call us into ministry, hold us accountable, and do the work alongside of us. Community is the first process through which God helps us to grow into our new names and identities.

Jesus formally invited twelve people to be his disciples. He intentionally chose the twelve out of the many who followed him. Twelve was a small number—insignificant considering the scope of the work, yet mighty and powerful in significance. It takes intention to focus on the transformation of people—taking the time to invest in their progress and growth. In this shift toward intimacy, Jesus demonstrates that attracting thousands of people with good preaching, entertaining church services, or big revivals is not enough to produce disciples who will be committed to living out the gospel.

Jesus desires intimacy with his people, and through that intimacy we grow into our identities. This is the second process through which God helps us to grow in discipleship—through the intimacy of community, organizing, skill-sharing, and prayer. As we come to know the love of God in Christ, we grow into our new names. In time, we are able to say with confidence, "I am a transgender child of God." Do you know that you are a beloved of God, named by the Divine?

The third process of coming into ourselves involves our work in ministry. Jesus sent out his disciples to liberate people with the Gospel, and that's how we all have had the opportunity to become disciples. In turn, we serve people through our words and our actions of solidarity—and as we do so, we grow into our new names.

In time, we are able to proclaim, "I am a disciple of Jesus." Faith is a verb, a healing practice, a direct action, a protest against the powers and principalities of this world. Each of us contributes to God's justice-making in this world. We must remember that our liberation is tied together and that as beloved people of God we must continue to fight.

Open your mouth and speak truth to power. Be with people who need support. Remind them of truth. Remind them of Spirit's unconditional love for all of humanity.

Ultimately, we are a people of liberation. May your holy name continue to speak liberation into the hearts of people around you. May we hold each other close, breathing life rather than death into this world.

As you do, you will grow into the new name that Jesus has given to you. We are the beloved community. We cannot be contained or constricted by the church or within the church.

My name is RJ. I have come to be a rebel and to resist. I have come to live and grow into the name my God has given to me.

Have you heard your new name? Are you listening for Spirit calling you to transformation? What is that sweet voice saying to you? How are the ancestors still speaking in our midst?

My name is RJ. And I am a proud Boricua, transgender, non-binary, prophetic being. I know I have been called by Spirit, by my ancestors, by my community, and by God. I am RJ, I have come to remind you that we are all divine beings and we are called to do the work of solidarity in the interests of liberation—to ask questions, to engage in community organizing, to educate and agitate, actively to seek transformation of a society structured to benefit a few, to listen to the cry of liberation, and to meet a God who is actually more like us.

May the Ancestors bring you support and pour forth their blessings upon you, your new name, and your new identity.

May you know that you are deeply loved, affirmed, and grounded in this life, building, creating, existing, and being.

May you know that your beautiful existence is resistance. Resisting the systems, structures, and powers of oppression. Resisting being colonized and harmed by the church.

We are the ones who say, "Not Today, Satan!"

The world needs us, and we need each other.

May it be so, in the name of Sylvia Rivera, in the name of Marsha

P. Johnson, in the name of gender nonconforming people, in the name of the Ancestors and the long line of Prophets who have come before us. Amen. And, Ashe.

Notes

The Reverend RJ Robles (they/*ellé*) is a Boricua trans non-binary femmeboi who found home in the South, organizing with QTPOC folks as member of Southerners on New Ground, community interpreter at Worker's Dignity (*Dignidad Obrera*), and part of the trans Latinx caucus of the Latino Commission on HIV/AIDS. They helped launch the Trans Buddy Program at Vanderbilt Univeristy Medical Center, a trans healthcare peer advocacy group that supports trans patients seeking access to transition related healthcare. They have done work on trans healthcare, HIV/AIDS, domestic and sexual violence, pastoral theology, and counseling. As an open trans Christian minister in Tennessee, their work has led them from grassroots organizing to nonprofits, hospitals to churches, and universities to community-led organizations.

Shea Diamond excerpts are from "Trans Singer Shea Diamond Moved Prisoners with Her Music While in Jail. Now, the World" by Chris Azzopardi (June 27, 2018, PrideSource), and "5 Empowering Lyrics from Shea Diamond's 'Seen It All'" by Henry Youtt (Billboard, June 29, 2018).

Suggested scripture

Mark 3:7–19—Calling the Twelve

John 15—Jesus and His Friends

Hebrews 2—Children and Siblings with Jesus

For further reflection

Have you ever felt God whisper something to you that no one else could hear?

Do you feel more like Shea Diamond stuck in isolation? Or, have you been able to find beloved community?

What dynamics get in the way of calling yourself a disciple of Jesus Christ?

An Encounter at Guadalupe

By delfin bautista

And Mary said:
"My soul glorifies the Lord
and my spirit rejoices in God my Savior,
for he has been mindful
of the humble state of his servant."

Luke 1:46–48 NIV

As I reflect on one of my favorite images of Mary, Our Lady of Guadalupe, I realize the rich complexity and beauty within the apparition of *la Morenita del Tepeyac.* Just as Mother Mary's radical "yes" pointed to God in Galilee; so, too, in Mexico on a sacred mount, Mary again points toward the Sacred—a divinely transgressive message that is still speaking in new ways 500 years later.

In 1531, a poor farmer named Juan Diego saw a vision. Mother Mary spoke to him in his Nahuatl language—the language of the Aztec Empire, native to the indigenous peoples of the region. Juan Diego was tasked with delivering a message to local church authorities and, in doing so, Mary's image appeared on his *tilma*, a traveling cloak made of cactus fiber. Even five centuries later, Juan Diego's *tilma* remains intact and is displayed in the Basilica of Guadalupe, where it is venerated by millions.

Our Lady of Guadalupe is an apparition that does not have one meaning. Today, she speaks to us on several levels. The apparition has social, historic, and theological implications with new discoveries and meanings to consider with each look at the story. Theologically, the story of Guadalupe demonstrates God's revelation through an unlikely hero, by creating safer spaces for divine encounter, and by liberating God's revelation from colonial paradigms—a decolonization that continues today.

As transgender people, our lives often cross boundaries; we transgress binaries and gender expectations as we live into our wholeness and embrace our sacredness by celebrating and expressing who we are (in whatever ways this looks as there is no single trans experience). Just as we transgress boundaries, the story of Guadalupe shows us how Divine Love also crosses over and defies the oppressive structures of this world to reveal wholeness and liberation.

Our call to proclaim gospel justice and to form beloved communities can lead us to moments where we must transgress, whether individually or collectively. We sometimes transgress legal boundaries, sometimes social expectations, and sometimes we even cross spiritual lines

Throughout biblical and Christian history, there are many examples of the underdog who saves the day. In Guadalupe, we see what God can do through the "nobody," through the outcast, and through the rejected. Just as God chose a poor, Galilean, Jewish girl as a way to come into the world in the first century, God chose a poor, indigenous man to reveal God's plan for a new creation through Our Lady of Guadalupe.

It is always through marginalized communities that God plants seeds to fix the mess created by the powerful—a sacred revolution that continues today. God does not abandon God's people but journeys with us, providing a message of hope that we are not alone and that the Divine can speak through all bodies, especially those on the fringes of society. These truths are reflected in Mary's Magnificat in Luke's Gospel and again in the magnificat shared with and through Juan Diego in Guadalupe.

In the stories of the Bible, Mary, Joseph, Hagar, David, and Rahab are examples of people who were not considered "hero material" because of their gender, size, class, or place in the culture. Yet, these lives revolutionized their communities and the histories of their people. Juan Diego emerges in this same tradition of humble, prophetic leaders called by God to reveal truth, bring about change, and reflect Divine Love.

For a long time, I struggled with the story of Juan Diego and *la Virgen de Guadalupe* because the story was lifted up only as a means for the Roman Catholic Church to convert indigenous people to Christianity. This belief system was imposed by the Spanish (and other Europeans). However, as I grappled with the image, the story, and its place in history, *la Virgen* assumed a special place in my faith journey.

It is no accident that God uses the language and symbolism of the "conquered" to bring wholeness and liberation to us all. The gift of Divine Love comes to the people once again through Mary, but, this time, Mary's image is Brown and speaks their language. This indigenous revelation deconstructs harmful rhetoric that would otherwise put European images and values at the center.

I came to understand that what happened in *Mejico* more than 500 years ago was a moment in which the sacred, the mysterious, the divine came near—a moment in which God revealed Godself in a way that Juan Diego and, eventually, I, myself, could understand, embrace, and identify. This has allowed me to embrace my messiness, my identity, and who I am as a person who lives *la lucha*, the struggle, beyond the colonized ideas of a Western worldview.

Misguided and, perhaps, well-intentioned Europeans came and

destroyed the lives of the indigenous people of the Americas (on every level). Native communities were flattened through a "salvation" by coercion and humiliation—all in the name of a God whose image did not reflect indigenous bodies or experiences, all in the name of progress, globalization, and evangelization. People along with their traditions, beliefs, and way of life were almost completely eradicated because they were perceived to be less human than the colonizers. European notions of God, customs, dress, and education were forced upon tribal communities.

Conquest and colonization did not give indigenous peoples the space to *desahogarse,* to unburden themselves, of their traumatic experience or to grieve the loss of their livelihood. Entire communities were treated like strangers in their own land. They not only worked, bought with their sweat and blood, and built homes on this land, but the land was also a source of connection to the Divine. They were violated and then blamed for being violated. They had no outlet to express their feelings without fear of retaliation.

This dynamic sadly continues today with many marginalized groups who are re-victimized as we are blamed for a dominant group's harsh treatment of us. Perhaps, we are seen as more human than we once were, but we are still perceived as a threat to be silenced (or again conquered). This is also a familiar narrative for trans people of faith. Many of us have been dehumanized by religious groups even though many faith traditions had previously celebrated those who lived, loved, and celebrated beyond gender and sexual binaries.

The story of Guadalupe reflects the need for safer spaces to connect with God. The church of the missionaries was not a place of encounter with God but, rather, a place of fear, pain, and terror. God's grace was not an invitation but an imposition; Christianity offered a tragic obliteration of their sense of self, their land, their families, and their way of life.

In the midst of this trauma, the encounter at Guadalupe happens. It is beautiful and amazing how Mary greets Juan Diego; her greeting in his language begins to restore the dignity that had been taken from his people. The apparition at Guadalupe provides a safer space. In addition, the mount of Tepeyac was a sacred site where the Aztec earth goddess, Tonantzin, was worshiped. So, Mary was also reclaiming this sacred site as a place of divine encounter, demonstrating that indigenous traditions and practices were not problematic or evil but holy. This is a sacred revelation.

Though the story of Guadalupe has brought healing and created a safer space for many different minoritized groups, I believe that the church needs to take further steps to apologize for its actions in the 1500s and not hide behind the image of Our Lady. The story of Guadalupe shows how

God reached out to create a sanctuary where there was none—where people could encounter the divine on their own terms and through their own unique selves, where they could begin to experience a new creation out of the pain of chaos and confusion.

This message has many implications for pastoral work today, as well! The story of Guadalupe reflects a both/and that recognizes both hardship and liberation in disrupting or breaking through any binaries that might limit the sacred. As a trans-queer person of faith with both indigenous and Spanish roots, my encounter with *Lupita*, this dark haired and brown-skinned woman, has been transformative, healing, and wholizing.

In other words, this encounter has made me whole. The image of *La Virgen de Guadalupe* was the first time that the Divine manifested herself in an image that was and is like me. Through the story of *La Guadalupana*, honor and affirmation have been brought to my *raices*, my roots, and my *lucha*. She appears as a marginalized person; she appears as one of my people.

God is with us in the struggle, *la lucha*. Juan Diego was on an errand early in the morning, when he received a prophetic message for the church and for the world. Both the *tilma* on which the image of Mary is preserved and revered and Juan as the recipient are important parts of the story. Both are reminders that the call to holiness is not limited to any one group, but is an invitation and challenge open to all people. Period.

La Virgensita is a source of hope and healing in a world that is divided by ethnic, religious, racial, and genderized "us *versus* them" polarities. She is a reminder that the Divine belongs to people of all colors, sizes, genders, races, and belief systems. By remembering Guadalupe, we also re-member the full dignity and worth of all people on the fringes of church and society.

God's complex and liberating revelation is revealed to us through simple means that still pack a punch. Through Juan Diego's testimony, the *tilma* with Our Lady's image, and guadalupen roses, God continues to speak to us today in a truly transgressive way. We sometimes get caught up in the grandiose and in the bells-and-whistles; we often forget that God speaks in the "still, small voice" (1 Kings 19:12 NKJV).

We are reminded that God can use anyone and anything as a microphone to speak God's message of love and justice for all. God spoke and continues to speak through the rejected and marginalized to the church and to society. While God's message *can* come through the institution and hierarchy of the church, it is not confined to it.

God speaks through the whole church choosing prophets from every level of church from bishops to forgotten *campesinos*. The message of Guadalupe did not come from a learned philosopher but from a simple

84

man eager to please his *dulce Señora*—the message that was given was directed from the *pueblo* to the higher-ups (not *vice versa*, as is often the case). God's revelation is bigger than the neat little box we try to put it into; it is not limited to one person or a select few.

Through this story and image, I personally came to know *un Dios*, a God with many names, faces, and bodies—a God of and in *la lucha*. *Un Dios* who is different and *unico*, unique—who is spicy, colorful, quirky, and transcends gender norms. *Un Dios* understands Spanglish, likes black beans and rice with a fried egg and banana, and can dance *salsa* and *cumbia*! *Un Dios* finds joy in widening the circle of *la familia*, enjoys a good rant about social justice issues, and finds time to laugh and be silly. This is a God who inhabits those in-between spaces of identity and expression.

The story of Guadalupe has multiple meanings and continues to speak to us today. I hope that we will continue to learn, listen, and live what Guadalupe said and continues to say to us today as individuals, community, and church.

¡Que viva la Guadalupana!

Notes

delfin bautista is an activist theologian and social worker who explores intersectional approaches to deconstructing oppression and lifting up dynamics of liberation. delfin holds a Master of Social Work and a Master of Divinity. Their background includes chaplaincy, campus ministry, case management, trauma therapy, faith-based activism, teaching, and diversity work in higher education.

Suggested scripture

Luke 1:26–38—Mary's Yes

Luke 1:46–55—Mary's Magnificat

1 Kings 19:11–12—God's Still Small Voice to Elijah

For further reflection

In what ways have you experienced humans who try to limit the ability of God to work in people of all genders, cultures, and backgrounds? In what ways have you seen God breaking through those boundaries?

How can Christian communities create safer spaces for all kinds of people to process trauma that they have experienced—especially trauma delfin bautista

that has been caused by church authorities?

What have been some of the unconventional ways God has spoken to you?

Transfiguration

By Merrick Moses

After six days Jesus took Peter, James and John with him
and led them up a high mountain,
where they were all alone.
There he was transfigured before them.

Mark 9:2 NIV

The Christ was changed before them
He was shining like the sun at mid-day
A miracle shared with devoted loved ones

His true nature revealed
Transfiguration: He is who He is
Revealed in the flesh

His divinity revealed
The True and Living
Acknowledged by Moses and Elijah

He is the Son radiant
Beckoning to freedom
By the revelation exact nature

Light beyond Light
True God from True God
One being with the Ultimate

Seeking wholeness we must become like Him
Ascending mountains of doubt
And valleys of fear and dysphoria

Our hope is to discover the Who to our why
We experience transfiguration in transition
By illuminating who we really are

Hidden in the recesses of the heart
We emerge like Christ from the tomb
Shining raiment of authenticity

Our truth cannot be erased
Our selves beaming light
As Divine examples of sentient life

Human flowers of resilience, sparkling nuggets
Of God's gold
Wrapped in the splendor of Grace

Imitating the Christ
Modern day miracles
Living and breathing transfiguration

Notes

The Reverend Brother Merrick Moses, OSB, is an ordained Old Catholic priest, urban monk, writer, community advocate, and teacher living in Baltimore, MD. This native New Yorker is a graduate of Morgan State University with a Bachelor of Science degree in Psychology and a minor in Spanish language. Brother Moses was one of the first Black trans men ordained within the Old Catholic movement in the Baltimore area.

Suggested scripture

Mark 9:2–8; Matthew 17:1–8; Luke 9:28–36—Three Versions of the Transfiguration (see Chapter 23 of *OtherWise Christian*)

Ephesians 5:1–2—Imitating Christ

Ezekiel 37:5–6—The Breath of God Transforming Our Bodies

For further reflection

Through your own life, how have you experienced yourself emerging as a more truthful and authentic representation of God's light in the world?

How does it feel to think of gender transition as a kind of Divine revelation?

Would you take a moment to celebrate the ways that God is breathing in and through you right now?

Unexpected

By Jessica Henrich

Oh foolish Galatians!
... Each one of you is a child of God
because of your faith in Christ Jesus.
All of you who have been baptized into Christ
have clothed yourselves with Christ.

Galatians 3:1, 26–27
The Inclusive Bible: The First Egalitarian Translation

When Apollo 8, the first mission to the moon, was orbiting the earth, the astronauts were performing a planned "roll" maneuver. Bill Anders spotted Earth rising above the lunar horizon and called it out. After taking a black and white picture, he asked for a roll of color film. Frank Borman jokingly told him that he should not take the picture since it was not a planned shot.

Nonetheless, color film was loaded and the well-known (and beautiful) picture known as "Earthrise" was taken. I keep this picture as my background on my work PC because it reminds me that, like the photo, my gender transition was not part of my plan. Yet, the unexpected and even uncomfortable can still be beautiful and enduring.

I have a degree in computer engineering and work for an aerospace company developing inertial navigation systems for commercial aircraft. I have also worked on sensors that help get probes to the distant corners of the solar system. I am a leader in a United Church of Christ congregation in Minnesota, and I have been married for 28 years. We have no human children, but we do have furry kids—a dog and a cat.

One more thing: I am transgender. I identify as female and use "she" and "her" pronouns, but that internal sense of my own gender does not match the gender that I was assigned at birth. I try to introduce myself with other things first, because when many people learn that I am transgender, they completely forget about everything else in my life. They treat me differently.

The people who get distracted when they find out that I am transgender reduce my identity to that one thing—to that one and only thing. They commit to every stereotype that comes with it. This shift makes it easier to dismiss or "other" me. I would like to be able to say that "othering" is something that has only started happening recently, but it has been around for many generations.

The churches in Galatia were made up of both Jews and Gentiles. The Jewish members did not want to accept the gentile members unless they first became Jewish, but Paul was having none of it. At the start of chapter 3, Paul admonishes the Galatians, "Oh foolish Galatians! Who has bewitched you?" (Galatians 3:1 NIV).

After some more teaching, he ends the chapter with:

> Each one of you is a child of God because of your faith in Christ Jesus. All of you who have been baptized into Christ have clothed yourselves with Christ. In Christ there is no Jew or Gentile, slave or citizen, male or female. All are one in Christ Jesus. (Galatians 3:26–28, *The Inclusive Bible: The First Egalitarian Translation*)

Paul is saying that through Christ we are all viewed equally and no one is more or less than anyone else.

Growing up, I just did not have the words to express myself about how and what I was feeling. I recall playing more with the girls than with the boys—from preschool to the third grade. They would segregate us into girls and boys at various times—for instance, at naptime. One night, I asked my mom why I had to go with the boys, when all my friends were girls. It did not seem fair to me. My mother informed me that I was a boy and left it at that. End of conversation.

Meanwhile, I learned about prayer in Sunday school. At night, my mom would come to tuck me in and we would go through "Now, I lay me down to sleep" together. After that one clarifying conversation about my being a boy, I started adding a silent prayer of my own each night, right after the scripted one: "God, please let me wake up a girl."

During the third grade, we had a school event where we each got to choose which of the two groups we would be a part of for a special luncheon. I chose the group with my friends. Of course, that was the table with all of the girls. Unbeknownst to me, the rules had changed. Apparently, the groups were supposed to be split according to (assigned) gender and I chose poorly. I learned this after being subjected to some playground "justice" at recess that afternoon. A shiner, a bloody nose, and a split lip taught me to be more careful. That was the point at which I went into the closet.

Soon, I was trying to avoid social situations entirely. When I did go out, I was really unsure of myself. In a mixed-gender group, I would wait until others set the tone and then followed whatever the men were doing. If I did not have a group of male peers to guide my participation, I would pick whatever seemed like the most masculine choices I could make—even when those choices made me really uncomfortable. I felt quite a lot of pressure to keep inside the boundary lines of gender in order to avoid being targeted and picked on.

While I was able to hide in many ways, the truth was not far from the surface. I remember playing Star Trek "landing party" with all the boys in the neighborhood. I was trying to fit in, but the group always assigned me to be Uhura, the female communications officer. Everyone else got a shot at being Kirk, Spock, Bones, or Scotty. They would even play the unnamed dude with the red shirt that would be killed 5 minutes into the episode. But not me. I was Uhura—every time.

My family was very active in our church growing up. We worked in the Sunday school resource center. I participated in confirmation classes, the youth group, and the youth choir. Each of these youth groups had retreats where I could expect to be bullied. Church was no different than school in that regard. My belongings were ransacked or stolen. I was also humiliated in other ways. When I graduated from high school, I walked away from both high school and church without regret.

Over the years, I tried various things to make myself seem more manly. I tried being a male chauvinist, but it only made me feel bad about my behavior. I almost joined Army ROTC, but realized (just in the nick of time) that the military would have made me even more miserable. I thought that getting married would finally "make me a man." It didn't.

My life revolved around creating and maintaining a facade to hide who and how I really was. I lived with a profound fear of discovery. Anxiety and depression were my constant companions. Any number of medications prescribed by medical professionals did not help. It took tremendous energy just to keep up the act—to make sure that I always reacted in the most masculine way possible. Eventually, it caught up with me. I decided to end it all. By the grace of God, my plan was foiled and I started to get help.

About 5 years ago, my wife and I wanted to attend a funeral in Fargo, but we had two dogs and three cats at the time. We hired a familiar neighbor kid to watch the furr babies. On the trip home, I found myself reflecting on the funeral service, which was a wonderful celebration of someone we all loved and admired. I felt inspired to pray for the first time in quite a while. While we drove, I asked God, "What do I need to do to find happiness before I die?"

Upon our arrival at home, I had a conversation with our pet sitter, who unexpectedly came out to me as transgender. They told me about their gender dysphoria and described the depression and anxiety that comes with it. I am sure that my face must have turned bright red. My ears certainly burned as I listened to a description that matched my own experience since childhood with an eerie kind of precision. It had only been a few hours since I had prayed asking for answers—for a path toward happiness. My prayer had already been answered! I simply had to start living my life as a woman.

God had answered my prayer quite clearly, but I still didn't like the answer that I had received. I started to read everything from medical explanations to transgender autobiographies. I was still hoping that I would find a different answer. It took me several months to convince myself that I really was transgender and that I should seriously consider transitioning to living my life as a female. I started looking for a gender therapist—and for a church.

I grew up hearing that God loved everyone, but there was a subtext. There was a "but." There was a well-known exception for "those" people. I was keenly aware that I was now one of "those" people. I had not attended church regularly since high school, even though my issue had never been with God. Still, I had lingering questions given my experience in the church as a young person. By this point, I had also heard plenty about the "clobber passages."

Soon, I found an United Church of Christ congregation in Minneapolis. I attended as Jessica, as a woman, from the start. Each week I went, the questions on my mind were answered in not so subtle ways through that week's sermon. After three weeks of such synchronicities, I was ready to accept that this was God nudging me further on my journey. I decided that I should join the church.

I was never particularly eager to chat with a burning bush. Nor was I excited to have a late-night angelic visitor trying to persuade me to "be not afraid." I came to this congregation thinking that I was unworthy of love, but the voice of God spoke through that congregation and helped me to realize that I was wrong about being unworthy. They quickly started to feel like another branch of my family.

A gender transition changes how others perceive you. It also changes your perspective on the world. In an adult faith-formation class, I was in a group with only female-identified folks. This was my first time in such a group as a woman. I watched in wonder. The conversation was like nothing I had ever experienced before. Unlike groups with other demographics, these women noticed my silence and invited me to participate.

When invited to contribute, I was caught unprepared and admitted that I had been focused on trying to figure out the rules of engagement. I had been too preoccupied to listen for content at all. Their response was to be even more interested. They wanted to know what I was noticing! The conversation shifted and we discussed my experience in the group openly. For me, it was the first time I truly felt like one of the girls.

Meanwhile, I had started taking testosterone blockers, as well as estrogen. The doctors said that, if gender dysphoria was the correct diagnosis, I should feel better within three months of treatment. Just four weeks into hormone treatments, I woke up one morning with no anxiety or depression. Praise God for guiding my steps!

Last year, I traveled to Phuket, Thailand, where I underwent surgery. Despite the aches and pains of surgical recovery, I had never felt more comfortable in my body as I did that day. I woke up from 10 hours of surgery as a girl. More importantly, I experienced a kind of peace and joy that I had never felt before in my entire life.

While my transition has gone relatively smoothly, my upbringing left me ill-prepared to handle the systems of discrimination and disadvantage that I now face because of who I am. In *OtherWise Christian*, Mx Chris Paige put it this way, "My white, professional-class, Christian upbringing did not teach me to survive in a world that does not want me to exist."

I first learned about systemic discrimination from a group of boys at the National Youth Leadership Conference held at a YMCA camp when I was younger. Unfortunately, I was unable to comprehend what they were trying to teach me. Their perspective was so outside of my experience that it did not make any sense to me. Now, I understand that God was speaking. It was just that I was not ready to listen.

God is still speaking and, now, I am learning to listen. In fact, being more comfortable with myself makes it easier to listen to others in every way. I have learned and am learning from women, from transgender folk, and from others in my life who have experienced marginalization. I am learning how to navigate the world in new ways, with new sensitivity to the ways we divide ourselves from one another.

I asked God for happiness. God gave me the blessing of inner peace. Happiness can be interrupted by a pinprick. It is fleeting and transient. Inner peace is something else entirely. It offers a strength that remains with me, no matter what.

The strength I have found in learning to love myself has been unexpected. It has opened up a whole new world to me. People like to say "get out of your comfort zone," but I also feel that I had to find my comfort zone, before I could really be ready to open myself to others. We do not always get what we want. Sometimes, we do not even know what we need without some help from others. Thanks be to God, for sending the unexpected.

Notes

Jessica Henrich is a lead software engineer for a Fortune 100 aerospace company developing inertial navigation systems for commercial aircraft. She does a lot of volunteer work, as a member of the volunteer board of a YMCA camp, as an elected officer in her church, and by mentoring young women for STEM events. She is married with only furry critters for children.

This reflection was adapted from several sermons that Jessica offered at local congregations in Minnesota.

OtherWise Christian: A Guidebook for Transgender Liberation (2019) by Mx Chris Paige is available from OtherWise Engaged Publishing (http://otherwiseengaged4u.wordpress.com) and wherever you buy books.

Suggested scripture

Galatians 3—Belonging in Christ (see Chapter 22 of *OtherWise Christian* by Mx Chris Paige)

Matthew 1:20, Luke 1:12–13, Matthew 17:6–7—Be Not Afraid

Exodus 3—God Speaks through a Burning Bush (see Chapter 1 of *Christian Faith and Gender Identity: An OtherWise Reflection Guide* by Mx Chris Paige)

For further reflection

Are you someone who feels self-conscious about social expectations and group dynamics? Or, are they something you take for granted?

How do you feel about the unexpected?

Have you ever struggled to love yourself? Have you experienced the difference between happiness and inner peace that Jessica describes?

Courage to Heal

By Yadi Martínez-Reyna

> *One man was there who had been ill for thirty-eight years.*
> *When Jesus saw him lying there*
> *and knew that he had been there a long time,*
> *he said to him, "Do you want to be made well?"*
>
> *The sick man answered him, "Sir, I have no one*
> *to put me into the pool when the water is stirred up;*
> *and while I am making my way,*
> *someone else steps down ahead of me."*
>
> *Jesus said to him, "Stand up, take your mat and walk."*
>
> *At once the man was made well,*
> *and he took up his mat and began to walk.*

John 5:3b–8 NRSV

As we look at the healing miracle in the Gospel of John, chapter 5, I want to invite you to see this story through the lens of the person on the ground. We have two recognizable characters, Jesus and the man who is said to be ill. Different translations say he was ill, invalid, sick, or living with a disability. In any case, this man is lying on the ground in need of assistance.

How has this person been there for 38 years? How did he get there? Did someone drop him off and leave him there so many years ago? Has he been stuck for all that time? Or does he somehow commute to the pools every morning, perhaps crawling back and forth from some other place of shelter?

This story reminds me of a time when I, too, was in need of hope, a miracle, or a friendly face to help me get off the ground. At one time, I believed I was nothing more than a glorified volunteer with no aspirations in ministry. I had been told that I was not only uneducated but also unintelligent. Those words broke me, sending me spiraling into depression.

I had been raised in a fundamentalist Pentecostal tradition. It took me a long time to find a progressive faith that would embrace my calling as a non-binary, transgender, Christian minister. So being told by these "progressive" folk that my passion meant nothing kept me from moving forward toward healing and hope for a long time. Like the man in this story, I was stuck and unable to make it to the healing waters.

This man in the story laid on the ground at Bethesda in Jerusalem—a place where there was a pool of water. When the waters were stirred, people entered, and healing happened. Some traditions say the water was stirred by angels. So, this was a well known place of liberation and miraculous transformation.

That need to find relief or support when we are sick or in pain might be something with which many can identify regardless of your culture. As a Hispanic, Latinx individual, there is always some family member who knows of someone who knows of just the trick to make it all better! We eat and drink all kinds of things, from herbs to animal parts, from soups to unsavory liquids that are said to have healing qualities.

We consult Walter Mercado, a Puerto Rican astrologer who many believed held the answers to everyday questions. May Señor Walter rest in peace, as he recently passed away.

We may look for a healer—not a witch doctor, but a person with magical hands who can give us a good massage, or a *limpia*, a cleansing, to chase away evil spirits.

This is a search for liberation from what ails us, by any means necessary. If I am told that drinking this water will heal me, then I will ask for a gallon. If I am told that this pool of water is a place of healing for those who enter, then move over because I am rushing in.

So this man had been waiting for 38 years, lying at this place of hope, waiting for his chance to be healed, but he can never make it into the water. Someone else always rushes in and cuts in front of him.

Jesus asked him, "Do you want to get well?"

Do you feel like it?

Is this something that interests you?

I wonder if this man anticipates the help he is about to receive. Did the disciples gather around him, ready to lift the man from where he lay? Was Jesus asking for his consent so that they could move him into the water?

Or, was the man by the pool cynical from his years in this place, thinking, "Who is this guy? What does he mean, "Do I want to be well? Is he seriously suggesting that I have not been trying for all these years?"

Sadly, I have heard people argue that the poor are lazy and should just get a job—or that immigrants are freeloaders. Transgender people are called deceitful liars, and the stigma for people with less-visible disabilities is similar to that for those with more-visible disabilities.

For those of us with more access to resources, it can be hard to even imagine the obstacles that can arise, preventing many kinds of freedom that we so often take for granted. Not every one has the ability to climb stairs. Not everyone has friends to carry us when we are weak. It would be dangerous to climb into the water if there were no one watching to keep him from drowning were he to slip and fall.

I also wonder if the people around this man had become comfortable stepping over or around him? Did they avoid making eye contact as they walked by? Over 38 years, had they stopped seeing him at all?

"I have tried," he responded to Jesus' question. "But someone always steps down ahead of me. I have no one to put me into the pool."

What a life! To have made his way to this place of hope and possibility, only to fall a few feet short. Healing was within sight, but still too far away to be reached. How discouraging!

In this story, we see a dynamic that repeats itself over and over again, even today. Someone is always stepping in front of the most vulnerable. The fastest, the strongest, the best connected are the ones who are able to get ahead, be recognized, and made well. However, the rest of us are not left behind for lack of trying!

Anyone who is an immigrant knows how it is to wait for that immigration lottery number, the lucky attorney call, or the long-awaited letter that finally says you have an appointment with a government official. It may seem as if you have to wait forever to get a permit to work or to study or to have your resident-alien status recognized.

In transgender communities, we also know what it means to wait for hope, for liberation, or for our own day of transformation. We call to make an appointment at a clinic, only to discover it will be months before one becomes available. Not many clinics are affordable, so we may need to wait in line, just hoping to be served. We wait for a mental health worker to provide a letter validating what we have long known about ourselves.

We may have saved the money for a gender marker or name change, but then we have to choose between moving forward and escaping an unhealthy situation. Sometimes, it is simply hard to make rent and groceries living on poverty wages or working in survival economies, so there is no wiggle room to save in the first place. It takes a certain amount of socio-economic stability to be able to set resources aside in that way.

Yet, this story did not end with despair—and neither did mine. The man in the story finds healing without ever making it into that pool! Jesus does not carry him into the pool. He does not push others aside to make a way. Instead, Jesus meets the man right where he lies and delivers hope and healing directly to him. No stirring required.

Jesus makes us whole by becoming our Living Water. We do not have to worry if we can afford it. We do not have to worry whether anyone thinks we are worthy. We do not have to worry whether someone is going to cut in line and take our blessing away.

Jesus has made forgiveness, grace, and love accessible to us all. He provides a path to liberation, but we still have choices to make. Jesus does not wave a magic wand to bring healing. Rather, he requires us to participate.

He told the man, "Stand up, take your mat, and walk."

It was only then that the man was healed.

We have to be willing to receive healing—but not in a "mind over matter" kind of way that ignores how the world treats us. Rather, courage is a very real part of liberation—courage to believe, to hope, and to act when our time draws near, maybe even after years of struggle and disappointment.

The man could have easily laughed at Jesus' ridiculous command to "Stand up." Why even try when you have fallen down so many times already? But, this man had the courage to try again, even after so many years of defeat and disappointment.

Thank God that someone also came to ask me, "Do you want to be healed?" Like the man in the story, I said, "Yes! But I have no one!" Yet, that moment of invitation opened me to new possibilities. It turned out that there were other people willing to help engage me in my own liberation process.

This brings me to consider the other characters in the story. For 38 years, there were spectators in this public place—crowds who stood by watching this man struggle: crawling, climbing, falling, and getting pushed aside.

"I have no one," he said. Alone, even in this very crowded, public place.

Have you ever had that kind of experience, feeling isolated and entirely on your own? Have you ever seen others look away in your time of need, refusing to make eye contact? Have you felt like a burden—like you were getting in the way?

Have you ever been like Jesus, taking the time to speak with someone others have labeled a nuisance to be worked around? Have you ever reached out to someone struggling with despair? Have you ever had the opportunity to look someone in the eye and invite them into their own healing? Or, stood by offering a shoulder to lean on as they regained their balance for the first time in 38 years?

It took years of therapy for me to regain my confidence. I worked with a spiritual director. I found a community of faith. I began working with a pastor who allowed me to serve with loving support and encouragement. Still, it took my seminary Dean Marshal saying, "I see you!

You are smart and you can do it!" before I took a chance on moving forward with my education.

Most of us have been the passer-by, at one time or another, looking the other way because we have more important things to do, places to go, people to see. Or maybe we have been overwhelmed by the needs of trangender communities, of immigrants and the undocumented, of the mentally ill or those experiencing homelessness.

We live in a fast-paced world where, if you are not careful, someone may run you over or push you aside on their way to getting what is theirs. It can be daunting, scary, and unfair. In such a world, we need healers, educators, pastors, and friends, who will look us in the eye and invite us towards healing and transformation. We need prophets and bystanders who will challenge the status quo and lend a helping hand.

I *know* what it was like to be stuck and unable to get my healing on my own, all the while feeling unworthy. Since then, I always try to remember that we need to create a space for *everyone* to find a home, not just a privileged few. All should be welcomed, regardless of their challenges.

Archbishop Desmond Tutu as having said, "My humanity is bound up in yours, for we can only be human together." and "We need other human beings in order to be human."

We are a community of furies, unicorns, little avatars, poets, dancers, students, and lovers of life. Small acts of hope and healing can be reminders that we are not alone. Our relationships matter. We need one another.

So, may we be bound to one another in love and hope. May we be transformed by the ways that we get to be human together. And may justice flow like a river and righteousness like an ever-flowing stream (Amos 5:24).

Notes

Yadi Martínez-Reyna is an intern at First United Church of Christ, Second Life, as well as youth pastor at New Church, UCC in Texas. They are pursuing an MDiv from Brite Divinity School.

This article is adapted from a sermon offered at First United Church of Christ, Second Life, an online community.

Suggested scripture

John 4—Jesus with the Samaritan woman

John 5—Jesus Heals a Man at Bethesda

John 7:37–39—Jesus as Living Water

For further reflection

When have you been most like the man in need of healing, isolated and alone? What gesture or support would have helped you find your way forward?

When have you been a bystander, overwhelmed, or unsure how to help? How can you cultivate the courage to reach out, not necessarily because you have the solutions, but because you care?

Have you ever had the opportunity to share yourself in a way that helped someone else step into their own healing? What did that experience mean to you?

Reclaiming: A Body In Prayer

By Bobbi Taylor

> *If we consider a spiritual path*
> *as a path through which we live out our lives,*
> *then we must bring our lived experiences along*
> *as we walk it.*

Zenju Earthlyn Manuel

I stand at the intersection of Zen Buddhism, Christianity, and British Traditional Wicca. All three are important to me, and each tradition informs and shapes the others as they manifest in my life. The liberal Christianity of my childhood brought me to Zen Buddhism. Zen Buddhism brought me to evangelical Christianity, and evangelical Christianity brought me to British Traditional Wicca. From there, I found myself turning back to Christianity, reclaiming my inheritance, and making it meaningful for myself.

Sometimes, there is a social narrative that a person can either be one thing or another but not both. According to this narrative, a person is superficial, confused, or deceitful if they claim an identity that somehow transcends familiar categories. As someone who sometimes makes the judgment and at other times is the one being judged, I am familiar with this thinking and its impact. Many of us face this when the question of gender comes up, as we are expected to "choose one side or another" ("So are you a boy or a girl?"). For some, such as myself, we also encounter these tensions with respect to religion and spirituality.

Within the context of my life, Zen Buddhism, Christianity, and British Traditional Wicca are all very important. Each has taught me a great deal about how I can navigate the world as an ethical, productive, liberated human being. These three different spiritual traditions are in dialogue with each other and find unique expressions through my spiritual practices and daily life. I take personal responsibility for what I believe and for nurturing this dialogue, even though many (especially from a Christian perspective) might argue that I should choose just one. I would no longer be *me* if I were to reject one or more of these traditions that have shaped me so deeply. They are all a part of who I am.

I have formal training in all three traditions and maintain practices in each. However, I identify primarily as a Christian—not to the exclusion of the other traditions, but inclusive of them. I was born into Christianity. It was the religion of my parents and grandparents and my ancestors going back hundreds of years or more. Even though we had stopped going to church by the time I started high school, the rest of my family remained firmly grounded in its Christian identity. However, I did not.

As I started to mature, I found myself gradually abandoning Christianity. Even the most liberal interpretations did not feel as though they could offer me safety from the homophobia embedded in the religion's core scripture. As a young queer person, I decided, quite consciously, that if the God of the Bible was going to banish me to eternal damnation, then I would live without that God. The math was simple and painful.

My desire for spirituality seemed to grow all the more poignant precisely because I could not find a traditional home for it. I was not able to find a community of shared belief. It was like being in a crowded room and wanting to find some friendly face—someone to talk with. Yet, I felt utterly alone, as if I had been shunned. Eventually, that changed.

My first deep dive into non-Christian spiritual community came in the form of Zen Buddhism. Although I had read about it in high school, it took me roughly fifteen years to find a *sangha* to join. While I was in graduate school, I began to develop a daily meditation practice and discovered the synergy that could be experienced in practicing with a group. I attended the weekly *dharma* talks, studied the literature, and eventually took the precepts, becoming a formal member of the *sangha*. For the first time, I was looking at how to live my religion in all aspects of my life 24/7 and from a perspective that valued clarity and compassion rather than conformity and judgment. And, I still practice Zen Buddhism with profound gratitude.

When my father passed away, I found myself wanting to connect in some meaningful way with the religion of my childhood and my family's spiritual roots. In a sense, I was still searching for home—a place where I could find refuge, connection, and a sense of self rooted within my ancestral heritage. This process led me to evangelical Christianity. Zen Buddhism had given me a deep appreciation for daily spiritual practices, community, and a strong teaching tradition. Looking for a Christian version of this, I ended up in a young, seemingly liberal church. I became a member and got baptized. I started to study the Bible on a daily basis and I joined several of the church's many small groups.

It was also there that I experienced a new way of praying. This was not the scripted ritual of saying grace before a meal or repeating the Lord's Prayer during a church service. I was familiar with that. This was more like taking part in a thoughtful conversation—silently or out loud, sometimes alone, sometimes with other church members—where someone would give voice to what they wanted God to hear. Then they would step back and wait.

It was this spiritual practice more than anything else that brought me into the evangelical world. Although I felt self-conscious at first, I gradually began to appreciate the fruits of this discipline, which often come in unexpected ways. I find comfort and wisdom in it.

For me, this kind of prayer is not an exercise in "ask and it will be given to you" (Matthew 7:7 NIV), as though God were some sort of vending machine. Rather, I approach prayer as a process that involves reflection, speaking, listening, and learning—then bringing it all together by living differently with greater clarity and compassion. The answer to a prayer can sometimes be close at hand, easy to grasp, or it might be the result of much hard work and introspection.

While the church's approach to prayer was opening new horizons for me, its approach to the Bible started to open old wounds. The church's culture of biblical inerrancy not only drained it of relevance for me, it amplified toxic social values that lead to things such as misogyny, racism, homophobia, and transphobia. What I first thought was a fairly liberal congregation turned out to be deeply reactionary at its core. It was antithetical to both my personal values and my well-being as a queer person.

Just as prayer brought me into the evangelical world, it also helped me leave. Burned out by the toxic social values of the church, I crossed a line where I started to swear at God, loudly and to express all of my emotions and desires. In short, I started bringing my whole self into prayer—not just what was acceptable to the church and not just what could be prayed in front of children. I started to pray as a whole adult—a whole, queer, radical adult. It could be as simple as quietly crying, "What the fuck, God?" Or, as clear as yelling at the top of my lungs, "Fuck this Christian homophobic bullshit!" I was not praying for divine retribution. I was authentically praying from and for my very soul.

I prayed my way out of the evangelical world and eventually Christianity altogether. I turned toward the world of Paganism—toward a spirituality that might be like that of my ancient ancestors, before the days of our conversion to Christianity. This was a spirituality that could carry us out of the darkness of night and through the seasons of life—a spirituality capable of making sense out of a world of diverse deities, diverse religions, diverse practices, and diverse human identities.

Having been born and raised Christian, belief in some sort of monotheism was ingrained in me as the one true path. Not only had I been socially conditioned to think of monotheism as the only truth, I had also inherited the idea that polytheism was constructed from the archaic stories of humanity's childhood. That said, monotheism also never entirely made sense to me. Even at the height of my evangelical period, the world felt too vast to simply be the provenance of any one deity. Human experience felt too diverse for any one framework or point of view to be sufficient.

Paganism gave me a way to shift from a monotheistic worldview to a polytheistic framework. It gave me a way to open up my prayer life to a larger, more inclusive universe. I would call out to the gods of my ancient ancestors, and I would also reflect on the deities of other traditions and spiritual paths—in different parts of the world and in different historical epochs. I began to pay attention to and explore the natural world, from the moon overheard to the plants at my feet, from the shifting seasons to the rhythms that flow through every day.

Soon my exploration of Paganism led me to British Traditional Wicca, a spiritual community where I could breathe, reflect, explore, and experiment. This was the refuge that I had been seeking—where people invited me to discover and re-discover myself. I began to conceive of my own body as both temple and altar, a place where the spiritual abides and is made manifest. I also began to question the gender that I had been assigned at birth. As I shifted from a monotheistic worldview to a polytheistic one, I also began to shift toward a genderqueer identity. I had never felt at home in a traditional masculine identity, but it wasn't until now that I felt safe enough to explore the question of gender and what it meant for me.

My explorations of spirituality and gender informed each other. I found myself inhabiting the world differently, feeling more grounded and self-assured. This in turn led me to the field of transgender rights activism. Working for trans rights in my home state of Massachusetts, I found myself confronting the very churches that I had once belonged to. I was now, literally, at odds with the Christianity of which I had once been part. Yet, this was also the religion of my youth and my family.

As with gender, I found that the religion I had been assigned at birth did not fit. I had walked away from it more than once, and now I wanted to take it and make it my own. Instead of abandoning it yet again, I decided to take ownership of my Christian heritage. I found myself wanting to pull it forward with me into my new life, to make it relevant to my life, beliefs, and values in new ways. Not to reclaim a church. Not to prove someone wrong. Not to proselytize. I simply wanted to go in the direction that I was feeling called.

I am a person connected with, informed by, and honoring of my ancestors. I also acknowledge the sins of my ancestors and the ways in which those sins have been perpetuated and propagated. Seeking to redress those wrongs and do things differently is a fundamental part of my path.

A crucial question continued to reverberate from my evangelical days: What kind of God do I want to work with? An abusive father figure? Nope. A God of oppression and injustice? Nope. Of fear and division? Nope. One that shames the human body, sexuality, and gender diversity?

Nope, nope, and nope. A God that calls for eternal damnation for any reason? Nope. That says some people are worthy and others not? Nope. One that engages in and endorses gaslighting? Nope. Geonocide? Nope. The list goes on and on.

For me, part of doing things differently is in the very words that are the lifeblood of my times in prayer and with scripture. How can I say things differently, in ways that bring my prayers more in line with my social values? How do I frame things in my mind and heart as I bring them to God? How do I move away from an "us *versus* them" mindset? How do I engage in prayer in a way that is fully consensual? How am I unintentionally perpetuating patterns of oppression through prayer? Who am I leaving out and dismissing? Who am I including and privileging when I pray?

The very term "God" raises these questions for me. It is so deeply embedded in the DNA of my spiritual language that, like a giant boulder, it refuses to be moved. As a Christian, no other term comes so effortlessly to my lips, and no other term points so simply and powerfully in the direction of my focus. Also, no single term carries so much baggage with it or holds such a profound history of oppression.

Redefining how I think of God is, itself, a spiritual discipline and a process of discovery. In so doing, I have begun to see that the God I work with is differently-gendered. The God that I work with is part of a universe rich in deities, identities, and traditions. The God that I work with does not deny the history of proselytizing and triumphalism of my ancestors but does call me to live differently, to eschew the cultural toxins that have infected and poisoned so much of Christian tradition.

I now see myself working with a God of love and compassion, of clarity, and of social justice. The God that I work with plays well with others. This is the God that I pray to, talk with, and listen for. It may be a different type of relationship from any that my ancestors had before me. That's all right. My goal is not to imitate but to discover and evolve.

Sometimes, to find ourselves it helps to find community to guide and encourage us in our exploration. At other times, to find oneself it is more useful to seek solitude. Clarity comes in many different ways, as does the "still, small voice" that Elijah experienced (I Kings 19:12 NKJV).

During this season in my life, I engage with Christianity largely as a solitary practice. I pray daily. Sometimes, it may be one brief prayer in the morning, sometimes longer or at various intervals throughout a day. Sometimes when the going is rough, I may find myself in prayer for hours. I also make a point of reading things that feed me spiritually—sometimes the Bible or another Christian text, but sometimes something else entirely. There is no litmus test. Every day, I take some time by myself to reflect and draw inward. This year, I also spent seven days alone at a retreat center praying, journaling, reading, and meditating, and it was one of the richest experiences in my life.

When I first sat down to write this essay, I found myself confronting two questions. Am I *really* Christian? And am I Christian *enough* to say something that may be useful to others? Both questions represent lingering judgments that I have internalized from others.

I know my theology is at times complex, at times fuzzy, and continually evolving—much like my gender. Yet, my faith is grounded in my relationship with God. This is the god of my prayer life and also the god of my ancestors. I may be a different kind of Christian than many have previously encountered, but I *am* a Christian.

I hope that by sharing my journey, I will give others permission and encouragement to reflect and listen deeply, not to settle for oppressive traditions that they have been given, and to open themselves up to rediscovering their faith, even if that means first letting it go.

Notes

When not in Boston, Massachusetts or elsewhere, Bobbi Taylor lives in Budapest, Hungary, writing, painting, exploring life, and washing dishes. They love coloring outside the lines, speaking truth to power, practicing what they preach, and discovering what they are going to do next.

The Way of Tenderness: Awakening through Race, Sexuality, and Gender by Zenju Earthlyn Manuel was published in 2015 by Wisdom Publications.

Suggested scripture

I Kings 19:9–13—Elijah Hears God's Voice

Luke 5:15–16—Jesus Prayed Alone, Frequently

Jeremiah 10:23–24—Jeremiah's Prayer

For further reflection

How has your spiritual perspective changed over time? Have you ever broken free from or reclaimed a tradition you were born into?

What does spiritual practice or prayer mean to you?

How does your spirituality connect with your body?

A Prayer to Begin My Day

By Bobbi Taylor

To the unknowable source of all creation, I give thanks.
From you I receive life and circumstances to do with as I will.

To all of creation, may I hold you sacred in my heart, words, and actions.
In ways known and unknown, we are intertwined.

May I never take without consent or cause harm,
but be grateful for all I receive and fully present in all I do.

May I be rooted in the ground of my experience and feel its solidity beneath my feet,
and may I embrace with love and speak for all parts of myself.

When faced with confusion and conflict, pain and adversity, may I find within myself
the air of wisdom and clarity, the fire of vitality and passion,
the water of love and healing, and the ground of strength and endurance.
And whether in times of abundance or need, may I give freely and love openly,
bringing comfort and pleasure to those around me.

In the quiet and the deep may I feel the embrace of eternal love,
and in both the light and darkness may I know and be true to myself.

So be it in this day.

Notes from the author

While my approach to prayer is largely unscripted, I like having one
that serves as a daily anchor. I began writing this one by reflecting on my
experiences with the Lord's Prayer (Matthew 6:9–13 and Luke 11:2–4).
Probably the single most important prayer in all of Christianity, it had been
an essential part of my daily spiritual practices in evangelical Christianity.

Using it as a model, I started by asking what I wanted to keep and
what I wanted to change or remove. For example, I wanted a tone of
reverence. I wanted to focus on my relationship with God and how I treat

109

other people. However, I did not want to use gendered or patriarchal language.

Then, I looked at what I wanted to add. What is so important to me that I want to focus on it daily and lift it up in prayer. For example, being fully present (from Zen Buddhism), never causing harm (from Wicca), and loving all parts of myself (from Internal Family Systems theory).

Finally, I wanted open and inclusive language. The result is a prayer through which I give thanks to God and creation and lift up values that are important to me. Although not explicitly Christian in its language, this prayer helps me deepen my faith by bringing together some of the most important aspects of what it means for me to be Christian.

Suggested scripture

Numbers 6:24–26—Aaron's Prayer

Matthew 6:9–13 and Luke 11:2–4—The Lord's Prayer

Phillipians 1:9–11—Paul's Prayer

For further reflection

Do you have any daily routines that help you feel grounded or connected?

From what kinds of resources or life experience do you draw your prayers?

Consider building your own prayer or daily mantra.

Womanist

By Diamond Stylz

Alice Walker first coined the term "womanism" saying that "Womanist is to feminist as purple is to lavender." It is a deeper version—a version that does not leave behind the poor or nonwhite, a version that does not just focus on equality with men. Being affected by an intersectional oppression comes with an intersectional vantage point for solutions, as well. Black women have never wanted a freedom that did not include *everyone*. When we work through the lens of Black women's experience, seeking to support the thriving of both cis and trans women, the world will change into one that is whole and well for any person inside or outside the binary of gender.

> For women who claim to be devoted to God
> should make themselves attractive
> by the good things they do.
> Women should learn quietly and submissively.
> I do not let women teach men or have authority over them.
> Let them listen quietly.

1 Timothy 2:11–12 NLT

I am in a "strange" situation that only God and I understand—and really that's all who need to understand it. Maybe some of you are, too. I was raised in the church. I try to live my life right. I pray for guidance on the right things to do when I am not sure. I work on my own salvation. But, if God let the "saints" have their way in my life, I would be sick, poor, homeless, or just plain dead.

We are far removed from the cultures of the past. Technology, socioeconomics, and science have propelled us far from what our ancestors were grappling with. The #MeToo movement, multiple waves of feminism, and conversations about a woman's agency over her own body are changing our culture. Women's power and our roles in society have changed drastically, especially compared to biblical times.

Take 1 Timothy 2:11–12. Ooo, Ouch! Back then, patriarchal ideology and rule was an overwhelming influence in culture and theology.

Like a women's feet after foot binding, people can be deformed when bearing up under a grotesque imbalance of power. Even the images of liberated women from that era were molded by deep-seated oppression.

For instance, Ruth, Naomi, and Orpah lived in a time when women stayed viable first through their fathers and then their husbands and even sons. Security meant surviving in the midst of the conflicts of men. Relative security from becoming a casualty depended on a woman's proximity to the men in her life. There are certainly remnants of those structures in our culture today, but women were much more severely restricted in their options at that time.

Meanwhile, men wrote the histories, so what they valued was the center of attention in the stories they told—men, land, and power. The ebb and flow of that power was controlled primarily by men, wars, and religions. In the Book of Ruth, there was a religious and cultural conflict between Moab and Israel. Naomi's family, which included her daughters-in-law, Ruth and Orpah (both Moabites), was a mixture from both cultures. This episode lands in an overall saga about how David would change Israel from a chaotic and decentralized kingdom led by judges to an orderly powerhouse under his lineage rule. Ruth was King David's great-grandmother (Ruth 4:17–22).

Meanwhile, Naomi's mission was to survive after the famine and death of her husband and two sons. This purpose would lead Ruth to Judea to marry Boaz and eventually to give birth to a son (who would be the grandfather of King David). But underneath this lineage of a powerful king, we need to understand that Ruth was taking unheard-of chances just to survive within the pressures placed on her by the culture of her time.

Ruth married a man from outside of her people, thereby disavowing the solidarity of her family of origin. She abandoned her national identity, renounced her own religious affiliation, and married a guy from the land with which her people were in conflict. The only person who was as radical as she in the Bible was Abraham, who also left behind his family of origin to travel into the unknown at God's command. Ruth did this without any divine intervention or human encouragement to support her in this decision.

Meanwhile, Naomi, an old woman drenched in tradition, told Orpah and Ruth to go back to their own people in the hopes that they would be accepted back. Naomi did not want to be abandoned further, but she knew how limited the options would be for any women who were without a relationship to men who could provide for them.

But Naomi said, "Return home, my daughters.
Why would you come with me?
Am I going to have any more sons, who could become your husbands?

Return home, my daughters; I am too old to have another husband.
Even if I thought there was still hope for me—
even if I had a husband tonight and then gave birth to sons—
would you wait until they grew up?
Would you remain unmarried for them? No, my daughters.
It is more bitter for me than for you,
because the Lord's hand has turned against me!"

Ruth 1:11–13 NIV

Orpah took Naomi's advice and went back to her family of origin. Ruth remained loyal to Naomi. Instead of going along with tradition and aligning herself with a man, Ruth chose loyalty to an aging mother-in-law. Her homeland was ravished by famine and her husband was dead. Ruth's story was shaped by her lack of options in that moment. She decided that Judea at the side of Naomi was a risk worth taking—and from her faithfulness was born the hope of a nation.

American culture has grown to value women more. The gap between inequality and equality has narrowed. There have been too many protests and bra burnings, books and think pieces, lives lost and minds shifted in our current era to go back to these old contortions of women's lives. Arranged marriages were the norm and have drastically decreased. We no longer openly stone prostitutes on the street. We do not have sizable harems filled with teenage women as a sign of wealth for kings.

As a transgender person searching for spiritual grounding in the 21st century, it might seem ridiculous to apply a text from such a distant time to govern one's life. Not because an ancient text cannot hold universal truths that will stand the test of time, but because our lives are so different now. It can be quite difficult to apply such a text beyond a metaphorical or mythical level.

Yet, I as a Black, transgender woman have much in common with these women. Three-fourths of transgender people have experienced some form of workforce discrimination. One out of four have lost jobs due to bias. These circumstances frequently lead to involvement with underground economies such as sex work and drug work in order to survive.

I was working in an assembly plant for Hewlett-Packard in 2002. I had just been awarded custody of my younger brother. My mother was caught up in the crack epidemic and the prison industrial complex. There was little sympathy for those impacted by drug abuse in that time, unlike today with the opioid crisis. The government was not giving resources to those who were struggling with addiction. They were locking them up. My mother went to jail, leaving my brother and me to fend for ourselves.

I dropped out of college and got a house on the south side of

Indianapolis, Indiana. Everyone in my family was against my getting custody of my brother because I was transgender. They thought I was a bad influence. This was ironic, because I had been managing the family since I was 11 due to my mother's addiction and neglect. I took care of my brothers. I stole food for my brothers. I hid the neglect from the school so that we would not be put into the system and separated. I took care of the household through many dark times. At no point did anybody in my holy-rolling family come to protect us.

Now that I was gaining legal standing to do what I had already been doing, it was incredible that these people were so vocally against me, a transgender woman, taking care of my brother. Despite everyone's concerns, no one actually stepped up and volunteered to take responsibility when my mother was incarcerated. So, here I was at 22 with an 11-year-old to take care of. I took on the responsibility first and foremost because I loved my brother. I knew that I would be the best person for him to be with for his care—and maybe I also had something to prove to my hypocritical family.

So, I found a place, I got a job, and I worked hard. I kept a low profile at work. I had a gender-neutral name even though my gender marker was not changed. Nobody usually pays attention to such details at first. I was working there for three months before anybody found out that I was trans.

Unfortunately for me, one of my grandmother's best friend's daughter started working at the Hewlett-Packard plant with me. Within two weeks she had revealed to everybody that I was trans. This started a month-long fiasco of pranks, disrespectful misgendering, and social isolation from the other workers.

All this chaos started to create a problem in the workplace—so much so that our supervisor brought five coworkers and me into his office to discuss the situation. At the end of the discussion the conclusion was that I was not involved in instigating any of the pranks or the chaos that was afoot. All of the other workers admitted to orchestrating the pranks and harassment. The supervisor verbally reprimanded them and sent them out of the room.

He told me to stay. In that conversation, he warned me that it would be harder to find replacements for five good workers then it would be to get rid of one good worker, such as myself. He admitted that I was not causing the problem, but still named the problem as my being who and what I am. He said that he would get rid of me, if there were any more shenanigans.

Only a week later another incident that I did not cause occurred. I was fired immediately. In the state of Indiana, trans people still do not have legal protection for workforce discrimination. I was devastated. I felt defeated. I was scared and unsure about what I was I going to do next. I went months looking for a new job as my savings dwindled. I was getting desperate.

One of my friends, who was already in the escort business, suggested that I place an ad in the local paper. My Christian up-bringing made me something of a prude. I had looked down on prostitution for years. I turned up my nose at the girls jumping out of cars. I would shake my head and roll my eyes when girls would leave the club just to turn a quick trick in the parking lot. I always considered them lazy or just "fast in the tail" as the old church mothers would say. I always thought that they just did not *want* to work.

I never considered the privilege that I had in blending in, even if it only ever lasted for a little while. Up until this point, I had always been able to get a job. I would always get fired for being trans *eventually*, but I would at least be working for several months in the meantime. Now, there was some type of drought happening. Bills were coming in, and I had mouths to feed.

I prayed about it because that is what I had been taught to do. I was doing everything I knew to find work. I could not go to any churches for help. All the church folks I knew were too worried about my gender to care anything about my well-being.

Life has a way of changing you. My conditioning to trust in God, prayer, and family was put to the test. Both my family and the church failed horribly. Still, I prayed.

The people in the community who everyone said were going to lead me to hell were actually the only ones who gave me a lifeline to survive. I needed more than a fable or a metaphor. I needed practical support from people who cared.

Like Ruth, Naomi, and Orpah, I was faced with a challenge to my survival and the survival of my family. At 22-years-old, all the things I had learned to do in my time of need were insufficient. The respectability politics of the church folk were of no use to me. I shifted, contorted, and adapted, like those women with bound feet. I posted an ad, as my friend had suggested. I came up out of that financial hole, and it set me on a better path.

I no longer saw the people around me as sexual deviants thrown together out of shared passions. I started seeing them as people who were seeking refuge in a world that was more than ready to throw us away. We found solace and support in one another. We found community.

Christianity is extremely prevalent in our culture. The Bible is often weaponized to condemn and isolate more than to embrace and affirm. That condemnation is particularly harsh for transgender people. It may cause harm in many ways. As an individual, I may lose my sense of Godly purpose and fall into self-destructive behaviors, while at a macro level

115

policies and laws cause or legitimate oppressive practices that may impact millions.

Affirming people is the key to bringing people into your faith without harm and trauma. So, if you are a Christian and want to reach people outside of your insular world, you must think of us as whole beings. Specifically, as a transgender person, my life experience does not revolve around just sex acts and sexual attraction. Our identities, our needs, and the families we make together need to be affirmed, if we are ever to find solace and spiritual grounding in the Christian faith.

Although the tongues of the "saints" wished me ill, I have not succumbed to poverty or hopelessness. I am really blessed. I have loving friends and family (even though they sometimes get on my damn nerves), a stable home and a job, good health, romantic and platonic love. I do have some wants, but my needs are fulfilled.

Looking back, my anger toward those fake saints distracted me. I could not even see how blessed I was. I am more mature now and weary of the battle to justify and explain myself. I have prayed through to conviction and received guidance and blessings in return. I can explain my unorthodox situation until I am blue in the face—and many people still will not understand. So, I do not bother with it anymore.

My life has a purpose. I am here and on this path for a reason. I know and understand that reason. When I need guidance I know where to find it. I will continue to sing my song of joy even in this strange land. I sing for strange people, like me.

Notes

Diamond Stylz is one of the premier voices of the millennial Black trans community. Currently, the host and producer of *Marsha's Plate*, a weekly podcast that centers trans-inclusive pro-Black feminism and pop culture. Diamond is also the Executive Director of Black Trans Women Inc, a national nonprofit that is led by Black trans women focused on social advocacy, positive visibility, and building strong leadership among Black trans advocates, activists, and our allies.

Suggested scripture

Ruth 1—Ruth and Naomi

Matthew 21:31—Tax Collectors and Prostitutes

Psalm 137:4—Singing in a Strange Land

For further reflection

Have you seen changes in how women have been treated within your lifetime? Have your own views on and understandings of gender shifted over time?

Have you ever had to make the distinction between making peace with God and making peace with church folk? How have you resolved such tensions?

Have you ever been embraced or helped by "strangers" whom you might previously have judged as dangerous or immoral?

Affirmation

By Dee Dee Watters

At various times in my life, I would ask, "If God knew me, why didn't God give me the right gender or body parts?" or "Why would God allow people to identify me wrongly?" For some trans-identified folks, they hated and hate the body they were born in—which is o.k. and totally understandable. However, that wasn't my case. Of course, I wanted to (and still want to) enhance certain things and develop in certain ways (as do many, if not most, people), but I never hated the body I was given. I just don't identify with the gender I was assigned at birth.

Before I formed thee in the belly I knew thee;
and before thou camest forth out of the womb I sanctified thee,
and I ordained thee a prophet unto the nations.

Jeremiah 1:5 KJV

God said "Before I formed thee in the belly I knew thee"— meaning that before the sperm met the egg, before the very first thump-thump of my heart beat, God "knew thee." God knew me! God also said, "Before thou camest forth out of the womb, I sanctified thee." To be sanctified is to be set apart for a sacred purpose.

But God! I *am* because God did *this*!

When I was younger I caught the West Nile Virus. I was told I would not see my next birthday (which was only a few days away). I was paralysed from the waist down, and I used a wheelchair for more than a year. For a long time, all I had was four walls, a light fixture, and a machine that beeped all night long. That experience changed me. I knew that I had to develop a relationship with someone—and luckily, that someone was

God. I developed a really strong relationship with God while I struggled to regain my health. God is my Alpha, my Omega, my Beginning, my End, my First, my Last—the very reason why I have breath.

I grew up religious, but now I focus on spirit. I believe in the Spirit of Love. Based on scripture, I believe that God knew me before I was developed in the womb. God had already set me apart for a sacred purpose. I was created with a purpose for love and understanding. I believe in God: I affirm God. I love God. I also believe in Jesus. I love not only because the Bible says I have to, but I love because it is easy! It is so easy to love.

Meanwhile, my business partner practices Buddhism. When his mother passed away, I went to the temple to be present with him. A Christian that I knew said that I was wrong for doing that, but I told them that the Spirit says I am here to love! It is a part of my ministry—to go to be with people who are hurting or struggling. I also feel called to honor and respect members of the trans community who have been murdered. My spiritual belief is love, love, and love: It's the easiest thing to do because I serve God and God alone!

I was 13 when I put on my first wig and started the journey of transitioning (which was put on hold while I was hospitalized and in the wheelchair). Upon transitioning, I lost so many friends and loved ones because of that. The people who I thought loved me unconditionally stopped loving me—and I needed that love! So, I started searching for love and affirmation elsewhere, but I was searching in all the wrong places.

I searched in survival sex work. It was the "johns" that made me feel loved because they wanted me (but that's *lust* not *love*). Still, I felt affirmed when they were seeing me as I really was—as a woman. They were telling me how beautiful I was—and, most importantly, they were paying me, which told me that I was worthy. No one has to know your entire story, but it matters when someone sees your existence. Being authentically seen is everything!

Survival sex work taught me things that no book could ever teach. I gained an understanding, like no other, of how life could change in the blink of an eye. I saw that no matter how much money, no matter how many johns, no matter how fine one may be, that each one of us women was an equal target for harm! Most of society does not care where we come from, how we look, or how successful we are.

I want for church folk to love and honor and respect Black transgender women by remembering Jesus. Jesus loved the "whosoever" crowd. He did not hold himself apart. He did not hide away with the "righteous" folk. He came for all of us. We need to be reminded about who Jesus really was—that Jesus was Love and that was that. We do not need to be competitive about any of it.

I was doing condom distribution in the Gayborhood here in

Houston when I found someone who had been beaten and thrown in a ditch. I did not even see her until I heard her moan. I brought my car back around, put her in, and took her to the hospital. She was beaten badly. Her CD4 count and her T cells were already low. The doctor told us that she was more than likely going to die.

She looked at me and asked me to call her mother and father. When I called, this person's mother gasped and dropped the phone. I spoke with the father and told him that his child had been beaten, that she was near death, and that someone in the family should be here. This man told me, "My son died the second he put on a wig."

It hurt so bad. Not because of what he said, but because all that hurt child was looking me dead in my face while he said this to me. All I could do was just sit there and smile. When I hung up the phone, she asked, "What did they say? Are they coming? You didn't even tell them what hospital I was in."

All I could say was, "Baby, I will be here with you as long as I can."

As a Black woman, I am aware that our ancestors helped build this society—and church was all they had. The men were out there doing a lot of the work, and the women were the ones who were building the community. I think about sisterhood a lot. Of course, not all of Black trans women are going to go back to church. Of course, not all of us are going to pray. But, we do need to figure out how we can get back together again as a community—and not just when somebody gets shot or when we are protesting the next horrific political incident. We need to come together in deeper ways as a community because each child matters. Every one of us matters.

Honestly, I do not nurture my own resilience as often as I should. It is something that I need to do more. I used to go fishing. That was my thing. I didn't even have to catch anything; being by the water was enough for me. I ain't been fishing in so long it is ridiculous. I don't even know if I know how to put the worm on the hook any more!

But, I am making my way through this world with God's help. At one point, I allowed people to identify me and define me. I used to seek affirmation from human eyes. Now, I know that I do not need that kind of affirmation from other people. Now, I have a clear understanding that God affirmed me from day one. Before I was even developed in the womb, God set me apart for a purpose!

I went from survival sex work to entrepreneurship. But, God! Yes, God has worked with me. I once was homeless, but now I am working toward becoming a homeowner! I was once paralyzed, but now I can walk and even perform. I invest in children with toy drives and other activities. I am a deaconess at my church. I work to affirm and rebuild our sisterhood. I want my transgender sisters to know that they are not alone.

As a Black transgender woman, it is my belief that when God sets us apart, it is for a purpose. I believe that God is in each one of us. I do not have time to worry about what you believe or how you live your life. But, I have faith in God and I believe that God is in you. So, I also have faith in you. If I have spent a few minutes with you, I am likely to tell you that I love you. That is not just my southern way. It is because I actually love you!

I thank God for loving me. I thank God for sending Jesus. I thank God for helping me make it this far. I thank God for you. Amen. Ashe.

Notes

Dee Dee Watters is a leader, performing artist, and unapologetic Black trans woman. She is an entrepreneur and serves as a deaconess at her church. Visit http://www.deedeewatters.com for a full bio.

Suggested scripture

Jeremiah 1—The Call of Jeremiah

1 John 4:7–21—God Is Love.

John 13:34—Love One Another.

For further reflection

Have you ever had an illness or other challenge that changed your perspective on life? What shifted for you?

What are some ways that you have experienced affirmation in your life? How have those affirmations supported or discouraged your reliance on God?

Is love central to your worldview? How easy or difficult is it for you to express love to others?

Finding Myself in Community

By Enzi Tanner

If I am not for myself, who will be for me?
If I am only for myself, what am I?
And if not now, when?

Rabbi Hillel (Pirkei Avot 1:14)

My Hebrew name is Ezra. My rabbi helped me pick that name because Ezra and I are both writers. My full name is Enzi Urimba Odongo Tanner. "*Enzi*" means "powerful" or "mighty" in Swahili. "*Odongo*" means "second twin" in Swahili, and I chose it as a way to be connected to my twin sister.

However, "*Urimba*" means "he is here" in Herero. That was the name that I was given when I was in Namibia. I was a Christian missionary at the time, before I had even started identifying as a lesbian. Gender is more fluid in some other languages. Being given this name feels like a really beautiful, prophetic gift that took me years to grow into.

To me, life is all about the search for my most authentic self, but it took me a while before I came to understand that things like gender or religion could change. At first, I assumed that these kinds of identities were static. If you were born female, then you must always be female. Likewise, I thought that you were either born Jewish or you were not. These were things you were just supposed to accept without thinking about them.

Eventually, I realized that just because everything started one way does not mean that it has to be that way forever. That was important because it gave me the freedom to explore who I truly am. Exploring what I am and who I am has also been a way of coming back into myself more deeply.

I see life as a journey. We all have different spiritual journeys—maybe there are even multiple kinds of spiritual journeys for one person. It can be complicated how all of the pieces weave together. For me, my gender transition and my conversion to Judaism go hand in hand.

The church I grew up in was the Church of God, Anderson, Indiana, which emerged from the holiness movement. I became a "born again" evangelical in high school and was active in my church through college, but they asked me to leave once I chose to withdraw from ex-gay ministries. After that, I found the United Church of Christ (UCC) and eventually the Fellowship of Affirming Ministries. I started seminary with the intention of being ordained in the UCC.

By the time I chose Judaism, it just felt right, but I am not sure I would still be here if I had not been rejected by those evangelicals. I needed the opening that the rejection created. It probably saved my life.

Becoming a Jew was an accident of sorts. Morning prayers were particularly meaningful to me. I was going to *minion* on Thursday mornings with a Jewish friend just because it resonated with me. Soon, I found myself in Hebrew class. Eventually, I realized that I was falling in love with Judaism.

So that is how it began. I feel like I was born a Jew—that this has always been a part of who I am—but I also made a choice to become a Jew.

Unlike the stories some trans folk tell, I did not realize that I was transgender at an early age. You might say that I was a tomboy growing up, but I was 24 years old and hanging out in gay Christian chat rooms before I realized that being transgender was an option. I saw the documentary, *Still Black: A Portrait of Black Trans Men*, and, for me, that was a really important part of my process—realizing what might be possible for my life. Once I understood it was possible, I chose to be transgender, to be a man, to be an intentional man.

Throughout my life, I have pushed and probed and found new language and communities that helped me to be even more authentic, but I have always been me. So, in that sense, I have also always been a man, and I have always been a Jew. Both journeys have been about finding a deeper expression of who I have always been.

These changes are like when I have gotten a tattoo. I never got a tattoo on a drunken whim. Rather, I would have this idea in my head. I would hold on to that idea for a long time, looking at it and studying it until it made sense. This could go on for years! I have always gotten tattoos when I was really ready—when I knew the artist and have the money and am prepared.

Transition was like that. I took the time to explore. Who am I? What is this like? Can this be me? Can I do it authentically? I realized that we are all on a journey and it is never going to end. So, I am always trying to figure out how I am going to fit into that journey.

Louis Mitchell coined the term "intentional man." In one sense, I am just being myself as authentically as possible, but there is also some intentionality to it. For instance, I want to be a man who is disrupting toxic masculinity at every turn. Love it or hate it, I have a role in how my masculinity functions. What does this identity that I have taken on mean in the world?

I think of it like having a covenant with myself as well as with my community. I am saying, "Here I am. I am a male (whatever that means). And, I'm also being intentional about how I do things."

For instance, I am usually working with female-identified people in the social work field. When I did outreach work, for instance, I had to be intentional about not wearing Old Spice cologne. I knew that wearing certain things would trigger my entire clientele! So, I wanted to be mindful. What am I doing? How am I going about this? How will people perceive me as I walk through this world?

I want to try to imagine how our ancestors operated before white supremacy and patriarchy. How did they embody community before capitalism got everything so twisted? How can I help to rebuild what masculinity means?

Meanwhile, leaving Christianity was also about shifting away from an emphasis on particular doctrines and beliefs toward an increased emphasis on community. Christians typically want to ask, "Do you believe in God?" I don't know. Some Jews do. Some Jews do not. I am not sure I understand God well enough to say that I "believe." Meanwhile, I no longer believe in the divinity of Jesus, but the point is that those are not even my questions!

I would rather ask, "Do you believe in community?" Yes. That is something that I can be sure of. Judaism is much more about community and about sacred space and time.

I don't think I am that unique. Some of my friends chose Judaism and some were born into Judaism. Some don't believe in God, but they are still very religious.

I find meaning in the rituals and connection of being in community. When I am going to bed or waking up, I know that millions and millions of people across time and across space are saying the exact same prayers. Some are doing these things at the exact same time as I am, and I know that it has been done before me and will continue to be done long after I am gone. It is so beautiful to me. I can find myself connected to community in a way like nothing else that I have ever known.

So, all of these journeys are also about community, and that is terrifying for me in other ways. I am an introvert who has really bad anxiety. I also deal with chronic pain. It becomes easy for me to become disconnected.

Sometimes, I miss services for health reasons. I know that I am not the only Jew at home wishing that I could be with community, but my body is preventing me from getting there. I think that it is important to give ourselves permission to exist within a time and space as we are and also to be able to get our needs met. There is nothing wrong with getting your spiritual needs met.

On November 15, 2015, Jamar Clark, a 24-year-old African-American man, was shot by Minneapolis Police in Minneapolis, Minnesota, sparking protest amid conflicting versions of the incident.

    I had been deeply impacted by the murders of several young Black men, starting with Trayvon Martin. Jamar Clark's death was local news for me, and I found myself stepping back from predominantly white community spaces as a kind of self-preservation. My stepping back was before Donald Trump was elected as the U.S. president. Anti-Blackness was not new in 2015. I saw many well-meaning white folk on social media, including those in the Jewish community, making clumsy comments about race and racialized incidents that increased my anxiety. I needed to put some distance between myself and the anti-Blackness and the white supremacy and the racism.

    People sometimes make assumptions about whether Judaism is good for Black people or transgender people, without recognizing that Judaism is more than a religion. It is a people. It is a community. It is a culture—and actually many cultures. It is a lot of complicated things all at once woven together.

    There are a large number of Jews of color, even just in the United States. Meanwhile, anti-Semitism is also on the rise. Folk are trying to figure out how to protect ourselves. Not all communities are good communities for me. Just as queer and trans folk have to ask, "Is this community going to be good for me?" Jews of color also have to ask those questions when we are considering a new synagogue.

    Jewish communities are wrestling with how racism, white supremacy, and anti-Semitism work together. So, we have to look at how all of that operates and not overdo it, one way or another. We all want to be accepted as our full selves.

    So, will you find support within Judaism? Yes, of course. Is there racism in Jewish communities? Yes, of course. Transphobia, homophobia, sexism? Of course. Will you find people arguing or even fighting about these things at every turn. Yes, all of that.

    Our community is beautifully complicated. So complicated that it can be taboo to talk about these things. People can be afraid to talk about it. We are just like any other family. We are complicated, and we love one another, and we have our issues even within the family.

    When I think about writing a letter to my younger self, I cannot even fathom it—because my younger self just did not know what was possible. It matters that there is more positive media representation now for transgender people of color.

We live in a society that demands more from us than we can give. It can be hard to explore your gender within a system that is designed to break you in every way. I am thinking of Black folk specifically now. It takes a lot of strength. Daring to explore anything beyond the norm can seem threatening. It is so insidious that sometimes all you can do, in terms of survival, is to toe the line and move toward your desire as best you can.

So, I want young people to know that there are adults in our society that do care. Sometimes, adults can figure it out in terms of gender and sexuality, but in many ways we have failed and continue to fail. For instance, we rarely support youth when they are protesting about problems in society.

I think we need to support youth, and we also need to step back and watch. We need to let them lead—because we are so messed up. Obviously, we have not figured it out, but maybe the young people have what we need. We have told people to be patient, but I can just hear Nina Simone singing:

I don't belong here
I don't belong there
I've even stopped believing in prayer
Don't tell me
I tell you
Me and my people just about due
I've been there so I know
They keep on saying "Go slow!"
But that's just the trouble

...

Just try to do your very best
Stand up be counted with all the rest

...

Oh but this whole country is full of lies
You're all gonna die and die like flies
I don't trust you any more
You keep on saying "Go slow!"
"Go slow!"
But that's just the trouble
"Go slow"
Desegregation
"Go slow"
Mass participation
"Go slow"
Reunification
"Go slow"

Do things gradually
"Go slow"
But bring more tragedy
"Go slow"

If you do not know the song, I recommend that you find it and listen. The lyrics alone do not fully capture the feeling that Simone portrays as she performs it.

I would tell the young people, "Don't be patient."

It is okay to tear up everything. If you have to flip tables to get what you need, then flip tables. Lately, some people have been circulating a meme that glorifies one particular protest because it was done in complete silence. People want to lift that up as the only "appropriate" way to protest. It is clear that they want to teach people to be quiet.

So, I hope that our young people will never learn to be patient. The system will just waste your time, one way or another, and the price of waiting is too high. They are going to kill us one by one anyway, so fight for what you need. Fighting can look a lot of different ways, but we have to fight.

Notes

Enzi Tanner is a Black, American Jew. Professionally, Enzi is a social worker working with families experiencing homelessness. When Enzi is not working or studying, he spends his time cooking or hanging out with friends and their children. Enzi believes life is a journey that is best lived through exploration, curiosity, and wonder. He has committed his life to community organizing in areas of intersection, in particular where issues of race, gender, sexuality, faith, and economic justice collide.

This reflection was adapted from a recorded conversation with Enzi Tanner.

Still Black: A Portrait of Black Trans Men (2008) is a documentary film by Dr. Kortney Ryan Ziegler, which features six short interviews with Black trans men. More at http://www.stillblackfilm.org/.

Nina Simone's "Mississippi Godamn" was released in 1964 on *Nina Simone in Concert*, by Doxy Music. Several performance versions can be found on YouTube.

Suggested scripture

Genesis 12:1—Abraham Goes Forth

Exodus 23:9—The Law of Strangers

Jeremiah 29:11—God's Plans for You

For further reflection

What kind of questions do you ask yourself when you are considering becoming part of a new community?

How have you experienced the tension between being patient with mistakes that are made in community *versus* pressing for change?

How has community played a role in your journey of self-discovery? Has being in community been helpful or harmful in terms of finding your true self?

Finding the Sabbath

By Liam Hooper

> *The whole of life is "a pilgrimage to the seventh day;*
> *the longing for the Sabbath all the days of the week*
> *which is a form of longing for the eternal Sabbath*
> *all the days of our lives."*

Abraham Joshua Heschel
quoting himself

> *And God blessed the seventh day and sanctified it,*
> *for in it God ceased from all the work that God created to do.*

Genesis 2:3
author's translation

> *And remember that you were a slave:*
> *and in the land of Egypt—the narrow place—*
> *the Existing One, your God,*
> *brought you out from there with a strong hand*
> *and an outstretched arm;*
> *accordingly therefore, the Eternal One, your God,*
> *commanded you to make the day of the Sabbath.*

Deuteronomy 5:15
author's translation

The commandment to "remember the sabbath and make it holy" (Exodus 20:8) comes, not in Genesis at Creation, but at Sinai. The Exodus from Egypt was a time of wandering in the wilderness, trying to find a new way to be in spiritual freedom. Both my own journey and my study of *Shabbat* have deepened my practice and understanding of this command. The sabbath draws me in and holds me, connecting my story, God's story, and the sacred liberation stories of our ancestors in faith—not only through repetition and practice but also through embodiment and breath.

There is a moment in Jewish *Kabbalat Shabbat* services—indeed, it is *the* moment toward which all our shared prayers have prepared and led us—where all the people, collectively, turn to face and receive the sabbath. These prayerful moments create a cathedral in time where all our longing meets God's own longing, the culmination of the six days preceding the first sabbath, this sabbath, and all the sabbaths before and yet to come.

The first time I attended a Shabbat service, some years ago now, those moments stirred me, like waking from an exhausted sleep. They stir me still, each Friday, since, as the light wanes and Shabbat comes closer to me, I move into the sanctuary of the seventh day. In this drawing near, I find repair of things I cannot always name. Increasingly, though, I sense that my relationship with sabbath inheres in my experience of it and the gradual, steady mending of long-held yearnings—for a fuller sense of selfhood, for meaning and purpose to the days of my life, for relational belonging in the world we inhabit, and more, for some sense of nearness to Holy Otherness.

Though I am by enthusiasm and affliction a theologian, I had previously never really *studied* the sabbath—that is until I *felt* the sabbath presence moving in me. I *received* the tenderness of God's seeking spirit welling into my own, filling the spaces left long in wanting. These incremental transformations led me to study. I learned that the sabbath resides in and finds meaning through the days that precede it. Through experience and reflection, I have come to believe that sabbath, with all the meaning it can bear, arises in our stories—not only, or merely, in the stories passed on to us *about* the sabbath but also in the stories of each one of us who has searched, or will search, for God. Sabbath is a cyclical time of discovering and rediscovering the Abiding One—the God who Abides with us.

As the story goes, God so longed for relationship that God set the whole process of creation into perpetual motion. God formed the heavens and all the worlds. God spoke into being the night with its many lights and the day with its bright sun. God made all the fruit-bearing and sheltering trees, all the seed-born vegetation, rocks, springs, mountains, and valleys. God fashioned all the creatures of the waters, air, and earth. All that is seen and unseen, God made. Then, with dust from the four corners and earth from the center of the world, where later the Temple was to be, Creator made us—temples of earth, blood, skin, and bone. Made from the earth of everywhere, the whole world was our home.

Then, God bestowed in us the gift of life, a living portion of God's own breath. The Hebrew words here matter. In Genesis 2:7, the first phrase tells us God breathed the *nishmat chayim* into the nostrils of this being made from the ground. *"Nishmat"* comes from the noun, *"n'shama,"* meaning breath, and therefore also, spirit or soul. *"Chayim"* means life. God gave to the earth-made person the *soul of life*.

Thus, by the end of the same verse, the earth being has become a *nefesh chayah*—a living soul. "*Nefesh*" means soul, self, person—biblically, the breathing substance, or essence, of a being. In other words, the story tells us God breathed a soul into the nostrils of the earth creature and (they) became a living, soul-filled being. To be a *nefesh chayah* is to be a living temple of earth and blood, endowed by God with a breathing soul—an identity, a personhood.

In that moment of creation, humanity took a deep, quickening breath and received a soul. We are reminded, with each breath, something of God's own self lives in us. With this soul, we were created into freedom, endowed with the ability and the responsibility to make choices. We were given a garden and invited into partnership with God in the ever-evolving creation of the world to come. The six days of evening and morning came to pass—and on the seventh day, God enacted *shabbat*. That is, God ceased (*shabbat* means to cease) from all God's labor and rested.

Mainstream Christendom makes the sabbath a day of rest, but, in this ancient story, sabbath is so much more. It is the rest that follows the sixth day, on which we all, through the first breath, were given a soul; it is the day the whole of creation—God and humanity, together—took a deep, living breath.

Shabbat, itself, is the collection of moments when we intentionally take a breath together with God. In Shabbat liturgy, each of the six ascending psalms is a day, an exhalation of gratitude and anticipation, leading to the next day, and carrying us into a brief remembrance of Eden. We are reminded, creation itself is the fulfillment of God's yearning for relationship expressed in enspirited utterances that compelled creation, breathed life into us, and continue to breathe within us still. Shabbat is the moment when we remember these breaths are God's own, inspired within each of us, exhaled and shared between us in a continuing, cosmic respiration of souls in longing—for connection to that which binds us, for rest, for renewal and refreshment of our deepest selves.

The liturgical movements of Jewish *Kabbalat Shabbat* service resonates in me—in a place beyond words and intellect. The movements of Shabbat liturgy link the practice of Shabbat to the first sabbath story, but, there is also a larger sabbath story in the sacred texts. That larger story, like glimmering Shabbat candles, illuminates just how intertwined the sabbath story and our own stories are.

If our lives are a pilgrimage to the Sabbath (as Rabbi Abraham Joshua Heschel suggests), then the conditions of our birth foreshadow or portend the directions and events of our lives. This is not predestination. Rather, like the atoms and molecules that make up everything that is, who we are and the movements of our lives come to be in a great cosmic dance of endlessly vibrating and converging dispositions, intuition, choices, and providential happenstance. All of the movements and meaning of our lives are seeded in our beginnings; perhaps, too, the meaning of our sabbaths. I can only say it is so for me.

On a September day in 1963, I arrived in the world two weeks later than expected. Undeterred by tardiness, I made quite an entrance. I was not only insistent about being born, I was turned the wrong way, with my shoulders oriented on the vertical axis. It seems to me a quintessentially queer-ish birth. Lots of energy, enthusiasm, and a little too much shoulder. In such a state, every contraction thrust and slammed me into my mother's pelvis, breaking my collar bone in the process. Still, battered, bruised, and a little broken, I managed to survive those circumstances and make it into the world.

Over time, I began talking about being a boy. This was especially concerning to my mother who was convinced she had given birth to a female child some five or six years earlier. Still clearly turned the wrong way, I persisted. It seems I thought people, including me, could sense who they are, who they might be, and make choices based on such self-knowledge. My persistence landed me in treatment with a child psychiatrist. I do not remember many details thereafter. The memories I have are mainly images, sensations, and emotions.

My doctors medicated me. The medication flattened and subdued me, impairing the parts of my brain that form, store, and retrieve memories. It also chemically dissociated me. After they stopped the medication, the tendency toward dissociation remained. I also received therapeutic instructions: "You are a girl; you will always be a girl; these things are unchangeable and you must accept them."

Other, more subliminal and lasting messages burrowed into my mental tapestry. Something was wrong with me. I would never, really, be grown and capable of knowing who I am. My instincts and knowledge could not be trusted. I learned silence and distrust. I learned to be suspicious of "help." My predisposition toward self-reliance was exaggerated by all the brainwashing. On the whole, I learned that I was incompetent.

This became my personal Mitzrayim. The word for Egypt in Hebrew means "a narrow place." There, I learned lessons familiar to those enslaved by the pharaohs of the mind. I learned to submit to the false gods of human arrogance. I learned to make bricks, build walls, keep my head down, and quietly blend in.

Thankfully, the body knows what the tender mind struggles to comprehend. The body remembers who it is. There were signals: sensations of dissonance and consonance, flickerings of light-filled insight. The self survives. I survived—though mostly dissociated with parts of myself lost in my own head. I was striving to cobble together a personhood I could live with, while over-functioning and trying to be invisible to avoid being seen in spirit and in truth. I would make bricks by day and dream dreams of a different life by night.

Eventually, I heard a freedom call; it was a young woman's voice. In those days, the world saw me as a female and following my attractions was costly. Again, it seemed, I was turned the wrong way. There were bruises and scars for this as well. While affectional and sexual attractions are independent of gender, claiming that aspect of myself was my first conscious, intentional step toward freedom. It empowered me to continue discovering and asserting hidden facets of myself.

When my parents found out about my girlfriends, they sent me back to therapy. There, I made the next pivotal step toward liberation. I refused to engage. I refused to be changed. Each week, I sat in silence. I had decided that if who I am is turned the wrong way, then so be it. (Amen.) Maybe this self is all wrong, but it is *mine*. By then, I had begun to understand that salvation depends on making a path toward an authentic way of being. I left a trail of pharaoh's bricks in the sand behind me.

I was sustained in this wilderness. It was still hard but far better than what came before. The more I followed a mysterious sense of spirit-smoke by day and desert-fire by night—a guidance both within me and, yet, beyond me—the more clear the way became. Manna arrived to nourish me. I was learning to trust there would be evening and morning another day in the constant cradle of something so much bigger than me. Miracles. Water from rocks. A tent for shelter. Surprising companionships. Love received. Love given. Resuscitation and recovery when alcoholism and despair, more than once, nearly killed me. The ability to turn away from the flow of common assumptions and expectations, to go another direction, may seem wrong to others, but it is in fact *a* right way. This willingness to be set apart may seem like aimless wandering. Only the wanderer knows it is actually the needful sojourn toward the self, necessary for all those who dare to be free from the bondage of the narrow places. This is what it is to breathe. Deep, renewing, liberated breath after renewing breath.

Though I appeared to be wandering, I was actually turning and returning toward myself—and toward God. When another pivotal night came, I was in my mid-40s. A yet unnamed illness landed me in the emergency room, near to death. The chaos of sounds, people moving, things being attached to me, and people talking to me and over me, triggered something. Like snapping awake, I came to a fuller, less dissociated awareness of myself. Suddenly grounded in myself, I saw my body as if I had never been there before. In a flash of bright, sorrowful recognition, memories flooded through me. I understood what remained to be healed. Lying there alone, I decided that, if I lived, I would give myself permission to speak openly and to accept and actualize my gender. I could see the fleshy homeplace of a promised land—a place of spiritual freedom, a place of sovereignty in body, mind, and spirit.

The practice of Shabbat prayers and candle-lighting continues to teach me how life is a pilgrimage to the sabbath. Now, I recognize that every step I made toward a fuller, more authentic expression of my self-understanding was like one day in the six days that create the seventh—the sabbath invitation to take a breather with God. I have discovered that, for me, resting in a more actualized sense of self is resting in the sabbath.

Mine is one story added to a string of ever-forming sabbath stories. Practicing Shabbat awakens familiar sensations of being accompanied that allowed me to find language for things I could not name before. It remains a sigh of relief—like the healing familiarity of being held by something bigger than me and beyond me, but also deep within me. I recognize the "still, small voice" (1 Kings 19:12 NKJV) that saved me in those piercingly lonely nights—the voice that lulled me to sleep, whispering softly, but firmly, "Hold on another day; wait until morning."

And, so, I have come to see my own story as a sabbath story. I understand and connect the metaphoric ancestor-footprints between my story and the stories of Jewish liberation, the Sinai revelations, and the wilderness wandering. This is the formational journey necessary not only for self-discovery and discovery of God but also for learning to bear the beauty, weight, and responsibility of all that is revealed. The first sabbath points a foreshadowing finger toward Sinai, just as Sinai points a hopeful glance toward the eternal sabbath in the world to come.

I now understand why the commandment to remember the sabbath and make it holy comes not in Genesis but at Sinai. Deliverance from Egypt to Sinai was less about a final, miraculous end to all worldly oppression and more about receiving understanding of spiritual freedom—and then learning to live in it. I had to learn this freedom—to choose and accept the invitation born in our first breath, to participate with God in continual creation of the world to come. Here. Among us. Spiritual freedom is indeed redemption, *teshuvah*, being returned, again and again, to the heartbeat-wisdom of our deepest selves, our souls—which is always a turning toward God, whose very soul-breath dwells in us and inclines us to the good, for ourselves and creation. The wilderness journey is about learning that freedom-seeking people help free others and the world—one freely chosen self at a time.

It may be true that I have been turned a *different* way all my life. And, I have, most surely, been left a little bruised and battered along the way. More than once, I have been a little broken. I may even be a late bloomer. Still, I survive—often against the odds and against forces much bigger than a pelvic bone. Yet, the more I follow who it is *in* me to be and become, the nearer I come to thriving. With this, I am assured that I am actually turned the right way.

On the Shabbat, I am re-membered and renewed—and, with each exhalation of refreshing prayers, I am reminded I once was enslaved and I have been delivered into the seventh day.

Notes

Liam Hooper, MDiv, is a gender theorist, writer, podcaster, theological activist, trans advocate, and educator. He lives in North Carolina with his spouse, Diana, where they raise their dog (Dodi), their son, and are surrounded by family, close friends, and a vibrant Jewish community. As he continues his journey toward Judaism, Liam engages woodworking, reading, and spending time with his family.

The opening quote comes from page 90 of *The Sabbath* (1951) by Abraham Joshua Heschel.

Suggested scripture

Exodus 13:17–18—God Leads by Cloud and Fire

Exodus 16—God Gives Manna

Exodus 20:8–11—The Sabbath Commandment

For further reflection

Does your life journey include a time of bondage, a time of exodus, a time of wandering, or a time of spiritual freedom? How do you honor those seasons of your life?

Are there moments when you have felt led by something mysterious or ineffable? Was it more of a "still, small voice" or a "pillar of fire"? How have these moments shaped and sustained your own journey?

What does sabbath mean to you? How do you find rest and renewal in the midst of day-to-day wilderness experiences?

Light Shining in the Darkness

By Z Shane Zaldivar

*The light
shines in the darkness,
and the darkness
has not overcome it.*

John 1:5 NIV

*I am a being of light,
bouncing around
in this vessel of darkness.
I am trying to let out
as much of my light
as I can
before this vessel dies.
I collide with
other beings of light
as we light up the world
together.*

Z Shane Zaldivar

I am not only OtherWise-gendered as a transgender man, but I am also an OtherWise Christian. I am two spirit. I am out of the box. I struggle to fit into mainstream Christian culture. I am committed to radical love, radical honesty, and radical consent. However, within those commitments, I am also playful. I am serious when I have to be, but even then I use humor, because that is also a part of being real.

I feel called to push boundaries. That is my calling. However, other Christians usually want me to pursue my calling the way that *they* say I should be. They want me to take an oath to uphold their systems instead of allowing my spiritual calling to dictate the rules and directions for my journey. I think that we need to be honest about why churches are dying. Churches are dying because they stubbornly stick with tradition instead of

139

embracing the living Word that they say that they believe in.

If Christ is our Living Water, then we need to move and change with Him. Water is powerful. A steady drip can break down stone. It does not take a tidal wave. It just takes time. Culturally and globally, we are in a season when things are breaking down and breaking open, but most churches have not figured out how to flow with these new break-throughs yet. Millennials are generally not concerned with binary ideas about heaven and hell. They do not even like worrying about if what they are wearing is "right" or "wrong" for Sunday morning.

I have a lot of questions about this "salvation" business. Often, it seems as though Christians just want to save me from myself! I am a person of Mayan descent. My people were colonized by the Spaniards. The constraints that most Christians want me to submit to seem like just another example of the ways that they have colonized me and my people. They want to take away my culture and make me more like them, but that is not who God created me to be. That is definitely not who the Great Creator is calling me to be.

Of course, they do not say it that way. They are more likely to say, "Why do you have to be so *extra*?" They talk about how I make people uncomfortable. However, when something edgy or unexpected comes up, they are eager for me to perform for them. It seems that they want to be able to pick and choose when I get to be my full, authentic self. Most of the time, I would rather be sitting in a bar talking with random strangers than sitting in a church building. There is usually more honesty and more Spirit in the encounters that I have there.

I was raised in a military family, which made for a very eclectic sense of community. Folk in the military come from all kinds of backgrounds, and then we get stationed all over the world encountering other cultures. Even in the midst of all those influences, my dad was trying to assimilate into this really "white" suburban life on a cul de sac with a white picket fence. We were trying to be "better" and I was supposed to grow up to be a debutante.

Because I was not raised on a reservation and that was my father's approach, I have really struggled with the pressure to assimilate. As an adult, I have been working to honor my indigenous roots and reclaim my culture. It can be a struggle sometimes. I told a Native mentor that I do not know how to "indigenous"—that is, "indigenous" as a verb. I felt as if I did not know what to do or how to be.

My mentor laughed at me. She said, "You don't need to have a *manual* on how to be Brown and Mayan! It's not something you learn from a book."

When the Spanish came trying to conquer the Mayan people, we fought them off the first several times they came. It was the diseases they brought that finally got us—first smallpox, influenza, measles, and tuberculosis, then malaria and yellow fever. One of the earliest Spanish generals became a Mayan prisoner, but he was so touched by the way the Mayans were living that he joined them and helped to defend our people against the next wave of *conquistadors.*

There are so many ways that indigenous culture is already "Christian." In Acts, the disciples sold off their land and property. They lived together in community. That is just how the Mayans were already living! We did not have to have a "Come to Jesus" moment, because that was already our culture. It was not white, suburban, capitalist Christian. It is also not "heaven and hell" Christian. Yet, indigenous culture is often "Jesus and the disciples" Christian. So, I see Jesus as an indigenous spiritual teacher who helps me connect to my Mayan roots.

I do not see Jesus as a gatekeeper. Jesus is just someone who is closer to the Creator than I am. I do not understand why people want Jesus to be a gatekeeper, deciding who is in and who is out—deciding who goes to "heaven" or "hell." There are so many stories from Western Christianity that just do not make sense to me. Where is the comfort in believing in a gatekeeper who might turn you away from the beloved community? I think much of modern, mainstream Christian culture just needs to repent and follow Jesus again. Christianity needs to let go of all of the conquering and converting and worrying about people's final destination.

It is difficult trying to explain indigenous values to people who just don't get it. This life is more of a journey than a destination. We need to learn to honor our elders and sit at their feet, listening to their wisdom. We need to let go of the idea that children are individual property, instead of a collective responsibility. We need to recognize one another as *tia* and *tio* and *familia,* as extended family members. To me, that is Christian community.

But, Western individualism is contagious, like the small pox and other diseases that they brought to us. It is easy to become isolated. I have to work to stay connected to my community to fight that settler-colonist disease. As a transgender man, it is difficult to figure out where to go for that kind of life-honoring community. I want to throw open the doors of the church. To me, that's what Pentecost is about.

I was in the Marine Corps. I resonate with Jesus in the temple throwing over tables, using a whip. One of my friends calls him "Combat Jesus." Of course, that image does not fit in with white, Christian "nice," but that is Jesus, too. I could never put my faith in someone who has not been in the same kind of situations that I have been in, just as I would never ask a junior Marine to do something I have not done myself. So, if I tell you to clean the toilet with a toothbrush, you know that I have already cleaned a toilet with a toothbrush before you.

I think about Jesus in the desert going through the temptations. I am here on this earth and I struggle with PTSD and suicidal ideation. I can take strength from Jesus because he has been through what I have been through. He has been through passion, trials, and struggles, as I have. He came out the other side, so maybe I can, too. I see Jesus as a prophet, as my brother, as my ancestor, but not as my savior.

I see our Great Creator in all things, as all things, constantly changing. That Spirit is fluid and it is all around us—taking the form of Jesus, the form of the wind, the form of our ancestors.

The deeper I delve into the Hebrew texts, the more I feel God there. I want to be like Nahshon, wading into the sea of reeds without concern or complaint. Nahshon was a tribal leader who was appointed by Moses. According to Jewish tradition, the waters of the Red Sea did not part immediately. Most of the Israelites sat at the edge of the water and wept, thinking that all was lost. Yet, Nahshon was that guy that waded in, all the way. It was only when the water was all the way up to his nose that the sea parted to make a path for them.

I want to have that kind of radical faith, following my heart and my intuition and my spirit. If it is for me to drown in the sea while following my heart, then so be it. It seems that white Christians are scared to have that sense of direct connection with the Great Creator. I talk with my elders and the ancestors. They walk with me. Much of what I have learned does not come from books at all. I am here for what is happening right now, in this moment, more than what somebody told somebody who told somebody several centuries ago.

I played the game of respectability politics for a while, and I learned that nothing gets done that way. I know that it is my role to open doors for others. We need people like me to propel us forward. I am going to say what needs to be said, because I might die tomorrow, and I do not want to leave unfinished business behind when I go. We have to get comfortable with ourselves and let go of everything else. I promise you that the minute you let go of everything you are free.

Notes

Z Shane Zaldivar is a Social Justice Warrior with 20+ years of experience advocating for marginalized communities. He uses his identity as a Veteran, Indigenous, Queer, Trans Man of Color to support all people. His calling has been to support those experiencing homelessness, and his specialties are suicide prevention and crisis management. When Z isn't advocating for the needs of others, you can find him on the Duck River in Tennessee connecting with Spirit/Ancestor or co-creating memories with his family and pack.

This reflection is adapted from recorded conversations with Z

Shane Zaldivar.

Suggested scripture

Matthew 4:1–11; Mark 1:12-13—Jesus and the Temptations

Exodus 14—Parting of the Red Sea

John 2:13–17—Jesus in the Temple

For further reflection

Does your understanding of Jesus encourage you to live in the moment? Or does it discourage you from living in the moment?

How would your life change if there were no heaven or hell?

Zaldivar describes "Combat Jesus" and "Indigenous Jesus." Also "heaven and hell" Christians and "white, suburban, capitalist" Christians. How would you describe the culture of your Jesus or your Christianity?

Doctrine

By Nick Manchester

Justice is turned back,
and Righteousness stands far off.
For Truth has stumbled in the public square,
and honesty cannot enter.

Isaiah 59:14
Christian Standard Version

In discussing decolonization with people over the past couple of years, I have come to understand that what has been common knowledge (and experience) in the lives of every Native or Indigenous person in the world is practically ancient history to most people of European descent.

The Doctrine of Discovery is a papal bull (that is, a holy decree) issued in 1493 by Pope Alexander VI. It gave explorers the "right" to claim lands as theirs for their king, God, and country under the guise of Christian evangelism. This tactic of Christendom dehumanized anyone who was not from a Christian nation, by deeming the inhabitants of "new" lands unable to own, sustain, or properly use the land they lived on. In short, the pope argued that indigenous people were holding their lands in trust until "better" people arrived.

This papal bull carried with it the expectation that Christendom would be spread to all people (in accordance with the Great Commission (Matthew 28:19). However, I am pretty sure treason, theft, and generations of genocide are not what Jesus had in mind.

It is convenient to imagine that the Doctrine of Discovery is no longer in use and has no effect on our lives, but there are many residual effects of this campaign, which have continued into recent years. Aotoria is called "New Zealand" because of this bull (pun intended). The original inhabitants of Australia (called Aboriginals), were only recently given the right to have standing in a court of law to get their own land back. In the United States, the Doctrine of Discovery has been used many times to defend the "innocent" and "harmless" settler-colonizers from the "angry" and "unreasonable" Natives. Even the liberal icon, Ruth Bader Ginsburg, has used this rule to contest tribal sovereignty, allowing for multiple treaties to be broken.

What does any of this have to do with decolonizing gender? I will explain the connections, but I need to ask that you keep an open mind and read with the intention of being better able to have difficult discussions with Native and Indigenous people in your own lives.

I am Navajo. My people call ourselves Diné. Europeans met with new people and, among nearly every culture on Turtle Island, there were people outside of the male and female categories, as Europeans understood them. These gender-full people were living openly and without shame. Some Native/Indigenous cultures had three genders, some had four, and still others acknowledged five. An offensive French term, "*berdache*," was often applied to those in these other gendered categories, expressing the scorn of the Europeans. This language continued to be used by anthropologists through the 20th century.

Priests came to believe that ridding societies of those that Western culture might label intersex, transgender, genderqueer, or same-gender-loving was the quickest way to Christianize the people they encountered. There is no "absolute" or "definite" way to count how many Native/Indigenous people were killed for being what is now considered LGBTQIA+, but the oral traditions of the people of Turtle Island, as well as the written records of monks, priests, and "explorers," provide a chilling look at these merciless campaigns.

The European explorers, armed with murderous priests systematically executed those in the "neither male nor female" groups. Within my own Diné people, the well-documented executions of not only *nadleehi* and *dilbaa* people, but also their children, show how these gruesome campaigns have been used to instill fear of intersex people in inhabitants of Turtle Island. Being both Native and intersex places me at the intersection of human rights violations, secrecy, shame, and violence—and most of this stems from the legacy of Christian supremacy.

Diné culture and language traditionally recognized four genders. Because of colonization, Indian Residential Boarding Schools, our ancestor's being forbidden to speak our own languages, and other kinds of genocidal behaviors, our language has been eroded, even as our people work and struggle to keep our traditions alive. Our words for gender are a great example of this dynamic.

My ancestral society is matriarchal, so our primary, or first, gender is feminine female, or *asdzaan*. The second is *hastiin*, or masculine male. Third comes *nadleehi*, which is similar to a femme man, transgender woman, or person with visible intersex variations, but quite fluid in expression. *Nadleehi* actually translates into English as "changing one." Finally, the fourth gender is *dilbaa*, which is similar to a butch woman or a transgender

146

man, but not exactly either of those identities. *Dilbaa* is a word that is rarely used anymore. While this is an ancient term, we do not know its English equivalent to provide a literal translation. This fourth gender is also fluid in expression. Many Diné use *nadleehi* for both the third and fourth genders, while sometimes we are broken down into five genders by dividing *nadleehi* into three subgroupings, including a more androgynous intersex variation.

As a child, I heard words in stories that described people or beings that I did not understand—and no one would explain them to me, as if the words were some guarded secret. It rather felt like they were saying "Shush. I'll tell you when you're older." Meanwhile, I was often excluded from certain things meant for girls, but I also was not allowed to join in with the boys. It made for a confusing childhood. I blame colonization for the perplexing way that my family tried to navigate these dynamics.

All of this is background so you can begin to understand my story. My grandfather was a Baptist pastor, and my father followed in his footsteps. They were both firm believers in the Genesis stories that describe the creation of "male and female" (Genesis 1:27 and 5:2).

I grew up knowing I was different, but the differences were not talked about openly. My memories are colored by words like "disordered," "deformed," "unsightly," and other insults I would not understand until I was older. I was not supposed to talk about doctor appointments—unless it was for the flu or something else commonplace and familiar. I was not allowed to talk about the appointments in which I was stripped down and gawked at by doctors, medical students, and who knows who else. There was a shroud of secrecy around my body as it was paraded around for all to see. I felt exposed and ashamed but most of all confused.

Part of growing up was going to church with one side of the family, who insisted that lying was a sin. Meanwhile, it was also somehow a sin to talk about my body or how my body was different. Asking questions about body parts and why they had to be looked at so often by the doctors—sin. Getting in trouble for not correcting people when they called me a "little boy"—sin. I knew I was a boy, even though my mom called me a girl. I could not understand her lie.

It seemed there was no way to live without displeasing God. God only made male and female, so then what was I? I could never get anyone to answer the question. This led to years of depression. I attempted suicide for the first time in my teens. I was 13. I had had enough health classes to know my body "wasn't right," and I had come to understand that the abuse I experienced at the hands of the doctors was not right, either.

I now understand that I had untreated PTSD and an anxiety/panic disorder that made me hyper-aware of my surroundings. I had no place. I was afraid of being touched. Colonization and generational trauma had made the more traditional side of my family homophobic (and interphobic, though I did not know that word at the time). The same forces had made the Baptist side of my family just as homophobic and unaccepting.

It felt as though Truth itself had fallen. My life felt like one falsehood after another. I was constantly trying to toe (firm, but invisible) lines in terms of my behavior. I had lost hope of ever making sense out of my place in the world.

Between three suicide attempts there were several rounds of conversion therapy. I was being told that all I needed to do was "accept" that I was a girl. Then, I would be "happy"! I was forced into hormone therapy that made me chronically ill, both mentally and physically. And there was prayer. So much prayer! "I'm praying for you" rolled off everyone's lips more often than I could count.

I was angry. I did not want these prayers. I did not want to "accept" that I was a girl. I was tired of it all. Life seemed ugly.

After my third suicide attempt, a therapist *finally* told me that I was not the only one like me in the world. Learning that the phrase "you are the only one" was a complete *lie* filled me with rage *and* peace all at the same time. Rage, because I had been lied to—over and over again. Peace, because there was finally some hope that, one day, I might meet someone like myself. My therapist told me that we were "incredibly rare" and that I would likely never meet anyone else like me, but I finally knew that others existed, and it was a balm for my soul. I would be in my twenties before I would meet another intersex person.

My therapist showed me Bible verses that I had never seen before about God blessing the eunuchs. I was fairly set against Christianity by this point, but I still felt relief at the words I was reading. It was as if I had been given a foothold between two worlds. Both sides wanted to exclude me. Yet, the Creator of those worlds had left a message for me, telling me that I belonged. Instead of making me try harder to fit in, these new revelations made me more desperate to discover who I was. I began acting out in a myriad of ways. I stopped stuffing my anger and let it flow—loudly and frequently.

It has taken years for me to understand the parallels among the mistreatment of Native/Indigenous people, the Doctrine of Discovery, and the violence of Christendom, yet the search for answers has been fulfilling in many ways. It has also opened the doors to help others understand the causes of their own generational trauma and begin their own journey toward healing.

As OtherWise Christians, we need to understand the basis of the erasure we experience in our faith traditions, but we also need to be careful to do this with love, compassion, and understanding, especially when we are dealing with generational trauma.

The time is coming when we need to seek peace with those of like faith—not by cowering, not by agreeing that our existence is a blight on creation, not by denying that God created us just as we are. Rather, we need to move forward, confident in the knowledge that we—whatever our race, cultural background, physical sex, gender, or sexuality—are just as God intended for us to be. In that confidence, we worship in truth and sincerity before Christ.

Notes

Nick Manchester is an activist for intersex, disability, and Native/Indigenous equality who is deeply concerned with creating equality within the LGBTQIA community for all, regardless of race, culture, disability, income, or occupation. Nick was nearly 40 before he met another chimera (his particular intersex variation) in person. He says, "It was overwhelming, as it is for so many who finally meet another with their same condition in adulthood." If you have been told that you are the only one, please reach out. You do not need to be alone.

To learn more about intergenerational trauma, please visit http://bit.ly/2TAZZ7z

Suggested scripture

Isaiah 56—Blessing the Eunuchs

1 Corinthians 5:8—Keep a Feast of Sincerity and Truth

John 4:23—True Worship

For further reflection

Is the history of Christian colonization something with which you are intimately familiar? Or, perhaps, something you want to learn more about?

Are intersex variations something that your family has been able to talk about openly?

Manchester asks us to keep an open mind. Will you commit to doing the hard work of learning what you can from available resources? When you discover questions for which you cannot find the answers, will you ask with humility and patience, expecting that the answers may not fit easily into expectations that you may not realize that you have?

Living at the Intersection

By Carla Robinson

While you also cooperate by your prayers for us
[helping and laboring together with us].
Thus [the lips of] many persons [turned toward God
will eventually] give thanks on our behalf
for the grace (the blessing of deliverance)
granted us at the request of the many who have prayed.

2 Corinthians 1:11
Amplified Bible

I grew up in Cleveland, Ohio, in a house at the intersection of 151st Street and Benwood Avenue. It was a great place to grow up. It was a wonderful house. Most of all, it was a great home.

However, living at an intersection is kind of a funny thing. I would not even describe it as "interesting." At an intersection, you have a unique point of view as you watch two roads come together. I was in the upstairs bedroom and my bedroom looked out over the intersection. As a budding young photographer who was just learning, I loved being up above it all— seeing people and vehicles come and go, seeing what happens as people mix and mingle.

I enjoyed that point of view, but it was also dangerous to live at an intersection. At the intersection where we lived, there was no stop sign. It was not unusual for there to be accidents. You could be sleeping soundly in the middle of the night when, suddenly, "BAM!" You would know that some car had rammed into the side rail or had skidded to avoid an oncoming vehicle—or perhaps did not succeed in avoiding an accident. It was dangerous and any given morning you could walk out there and find the remains of an accident, with broken glass and shredded metal all over your front lawn. Of course, you needed to be careful trying to cross the street.

Living at the intersection of 151st Street and Benwood Avenue also meant a lot more work than some of our other neighbors. We were on the corner, and that meant we had a longer tree line which brought more raking of the leaves in the fall. Being at an intersection meant that we had a longer sidewalk that brought more shoveling of snow in the winter. Being on a corner lot meant a larger lawn to mow in the spring and in the summer. It was more work, all the time!

Yet, living at the intersection also meant that we had some opportunities. That nice long tree line meant additional trees for climbing children to play in. Those long sidewalks meant a nice ride around the curve on your bicycle. The yard of that nice big corner lot meant lots of room to run through sprinklers on hot days in northeastern Ohio.

Living at an intersection brings you a point of view and some danger. It also brings you additional work and opportunities. I have not lived in that house in many years, but I still live at an intersection. These days, I live at the intersection of Transgender Street and Black Boulevard. As with the intersection where I grew up, there is a point of view and danger. There are also additional work and opportunities.

The danger there is real. To be Black in America means that you are at a higher risk to be incarcerated, a higher risk to experience brutality at the hands of law enforcement, a higher risk to die of heart disease, a higher risk to die of the complications of diabetes, a higher risk to live in poverty, a higher risk to have no health care, a higher risk to be homeless, a higher risk to die from the complications of diseases that could be prevented. All this and there is also a higher risk of being unemployed or underemployed, a higher risk of being evicted, a higher risk of watching one's family members die in front of one's very eyes. It is still dangerous to be Black in America.

On top of all that, I am transgender *and* Black in America. You can *double* all of those statistics. You can add in higher risk to die of sexually transmitted disease, higher risk to be ignored by the healthcare system, higher risk to be killed or murdered in a torturous manner on the streets of your own hometown. There is plenty of danger at the intersection of Transgender Street and Black Boulevard—even now in the twenty-first century.

But, those of us who are living at this intersection are not the only ones in danger. You are in danger, too. If you are listening to me today and you are in any way shape or form connected with society in the United States, you are in danger, too. It is the danger that comes from knowing what you now know—that there are those living in the midst of injustice right in the shadow of *your* home.

You are in danger of not acting. You are in danger of a spiritual complacency, because many of you keep closing your eyes so you don't have to think about it.

You might say, "I'm not Black and I don't worry about that" or you can might say, "I'm not trans and I don't have to worry about that." You can sit back and be comfortable and cool and safe navigating the world without those concerns. However, that approach is dangerous. It breeds a complacency that may grow. Complacency can keep you from acting in the way that you know you should as someone connected to Jesus. That is the danger.

As Dr. King reminded us: "If even one of us is not free, all of us are not free." You and I are, in the biblical sense, neighbors. In the deeper biblical sense, we are kinfolk to each other, regardless of where we come from or how we identify in terms of gender. We are in danger if we do not act.

Living at the intersection of Transgender Street and Black Boulevard also means that there is a unique point of view. From where I stand, I can look at the Black community from the transgender community, and I can look at the transgender community from the Black community. I can also look at the outside world from both communities. It is the point of view that helps me see injustice in a very clear light.

Sometimes, that means I have to call my communities to accountability. I have to say to my Black sisters and brothers, we must never be among those who oppress folk because of their gender identity, because they are transgender, because they are gender nonconforming. We must never fall into that trap because we ourselves have been condemned for who we are.

I have to sometimes say to my transgender siblings, we cannot dare abide racism in our community. We must stand against it because we have been discriminated against, too.

I look out on a wider society, knowing firsthand how damaging and destructive racism and transmisogyny can be. Come stand near me. Listen to what my life is like. Listen to what I go through, so you, too, can see things in a different light.

You do that by listening to me, by being in conversation with me as we exchange our stories about what our daily life is like. You will never be able to stand in my shoes, but you will stand next to my shoes and see a little bit of the world from my point of view. Perhaps your eyes will be opened to see injustices that you did not see before. Perhaps your heart will be stirred to say, "This must *not* continue! This is not the way God desires God's children to be living."

At the intersection of Transgender Street and Black Boulevard, there is a lot of work to be done. Yes, a lot! My dad taught us when we were coming up about the "two-and-a-half rule." It goes like this: Being Black in America means you have to work twice as hard to get half as far. It is unjust, but it is a reality.

When I go into a job interview, when I walk into a store, when I go to buy a coffee, when I step into a church, part of what I have to deal with is the fact that people may have preconceived ideas about me. I may walk into a particular church and people may say, "Oh, I see it's a Black person, and she won't know what this particular church is about." They may draw a conclusion about what my education level is or what my interests will be or how hard I will work. They may have assumptions about how I will speak and how I will dress, too. I have got to deal with all of these things before I even open my mouth!

It is part of my work to clear some kind of a space so that maybe an individual can see me as *Carla* who also happens to be Black and transgender.

There is also extra work to be transgender in America. I have to worry about how healthcare is going to treat me, what the doctor is going to say when I have to go to the emergency room, what is going to happen when I have to go to a new place and I have to go to the bathroom. I have to worry when I am being interviewed, if I might not get the job because the work culture there was uncomfortable with trans people. I have to wonder if TSA is going to be a problem when I travel on a commercial airline. These kinds of things are a part of my daily life. Even more than that, if something goes wrong and something crazy happens, what jail will they throw me into?

So, I present myself to the world in ways that I hope will clear away some of these prejudices, so I can be seen as Carla who is Black and transgender. It is a constant effort. It is work all of the time. If you ask most Black folk and most transgender folk how they feel (and if we are honest), we will tell you that most of the time we are tired, just because it is so much work.

But, there is work for you, too! You may not be Black and you may not be transgender, but there is work for you, because *I* am living at the intersection of Transgender Street and Black Boulevard. The work for you is the work of understanding. The work for you is the work of coming alongside me and being an ally with me. The work for you is discerning what it looks like for you to use your position and your access to further *my* freedom. Part of the work that you need to do is figuring out how to stand, how to make the changes that you know are necessary, so that life at the intersection of Transgender Street and Black Boulevard can be full, free, and beautiful.

If you are a doctor, what does that mean? For a nurse, what might you do? If you are in government, what does that mean for you? What if you work in the school district? What if you have some of the most holy work of all? If you are raising a child, you hold the future in your hands—as you shape a child to know that all God's children are deeply loved by God. All God's children are worthy of respect. All God's children have dignity. All God's children are beautiful creatures of the Almighty, endowed with the very image of God. This is the work that you and I are called to do together.

Finally, there is also opportunity at this intersection. All is not grim. All is not danger. All is not pain. All is not tears at the intersection of Transgender Street and Black Boulevard. There are opportunities for connection and for friendship. There are opportunities to have our hearts and minds broken open, for new things to be poured into us.

When I was first wrestling with what it means to be transgender and I was just starting to come out, one of the things I was afraid of was rejection. I was afraid my family would reject me. I was afraid my friends would reject me. I was afraid my church would reject me.

Well, my church did reject me, and many of my friends did abandon me, but my family not only stayed, they changed. We all changed, actually. We found out that love can show up in new ways. We found out that love can persist even when people are going through the most disorienting changes we have ever seen! We discovered just how strong love is, and we discovered what was important to us.

My mama told me "You were my child. God gave me to you and I have no intention of letting you go." Then she lived it. She took her understanding of the love of God and applied it to the idea that one of her children was transgender. When she applied God's love to this situation, she came out with something that Jesus said a long time ago, "love one another as I have loved you" (John 13:34 NIV).

That is the opportunity that we all have at the intersection of Transgender Street and Black Boulevard: The opportunity to see love take new shapes, to see love morph and become something deeper and greater than we thought it could be! That is the opportunity that keeps me going.

When I look at the pain that comes from living at that intersection, I sometimes get discouraged, but then I remember the opportunity; and I remember what Jesus showed us. You just watch love do its thing!

We can change life at the intersection of Transgender Street and Black Boulevard. We can change it. We have the power by God's Spirit to combat the combined sins of racism and transmisogyny. We can do that. We have that opportunity now more than at any other time before. Thanks to technology and books like this, we can connect with one another now more than ever.

I love that we have these kinds of opportunities to reach one another in ways that we never could have before. We have a chance to form alliances across denominational lines, across faith lines, across political lines, across economic lines. We have the opportunity to transform life at the intersection of Transgender Street and Black Boulevard. We have the opportunity, and we have the power.

Why not do it now? If not now, when? If not us, who? Dr. King said, "The arc of the moral universe is long, but it bends toward justice." In saying that what he meant was our work may not be completed quickly or easily, but it will bend toward justice. It will bend that way because we are going to grab hold of that arc and not let go! And, because there are stronger hands than ours that also hold that arc.

Life at an intersection is interesting. I live at that intersection. Won't you visit me frequently? I would love to tell you more about life there: the dangers, the point of view, the work, and the opportunity. Let's walk together. Shall we?

Notes

The Reverend Carla Robinson, a graduate of Concordia Seminary (St. Louis, Missouri), served as a Lutheran pastor for 13 years before coming to the Episcopal Church. She was received into the Anglican Communion in 2001. She has served as the Administrative Assistant for Multi-Cultural Ministry and the Secretary for Vocations in the Diocese of Olympia. Since her ordination in 2009, she has served several parishes. She currently serves as associate priest at Christ Church in Seattle's University District.

This reflection is adapted from a sermon, "Living at the Intersection of Transgender Street and Black Boulevard," preached by the Robinson on February 10, 2019 for Welcome Table Christian Church (Seattle, Washington). Available at https://www.youtube.com/watch?v=41vDg2u_vrk.

The quote from the Reverend Dr. Martin Luther King, Jr was from his 1964 Baccalaureate sermon at the commencement exercises for Wesleyan University in Middletown, Connecticut. It is considered a paraphrase of comments from Theodore Parker in a sermon published in 1853.

Suggested scripture

Luke 10:30–33—Love Your Neighbor

John 13:34, 15:12—Love One Another, As I Have Loved You

Hebrews 13:1—Love One Another As Siblings

For further reflection

What intersections do *you* live at? Does it make you tired?

Have you ever had the experience of visiting someone "where they live" and learned something about yourself?

How might you refocus your efforts in light of the testimonies you have read in *OtherWise Christian 2: Stories of Resistance*?

Section 3

Resisting the Stories
They Tell about Us

Resurrected Bodies

By Lianne Simon

And if the Spirit of him
who raised Jesus from the dead
is living in you,
he who raised Christ from the dead
will also give life to your mortal bodies
because of his Spirit who lives in you.

Romans 8:11 NIV

Sex and gender are certainly a large part of who we are. But because I have an intersex variation—my body is not entirely male or female—I am often puzzled by the statements some Christians make regarding theological issues involving the human body.

Quite a few Christians insist that, in the Resurrection, we will not only be male or female, but that the male-female binary will be perfect. Intersex variations will not exist. Recent conversations regarding the resurrection of the dead have caused me to further examine, not only my own views on the subject, but my life as an intersex woman.

When I started living as a girl, my mother told me that, for the first time in my life, she knew I would be okay. As a parent, she supported me, but as a Christian, she wondered how I would spend eternity. In other words, would her intersex child be a boy or a girl in heaven?

I told her that I was not certain how to answer her question, but I knew that my Redeemer loved me, and that was enough for me. Nothing was impossible for God.

And I am sure of this,
that he who began a good work in you
will bring it to completion
at the day of Jesus Christ.

Philippians 1:6 ESV

My body is intersex. I have a condition called Mixed Gonadal Dysgenesis. Some of my cells have a Y chromosome; others do not. That resulted in my having a mix of ovarian and testicular tissue as well as a number of other medical issues. Although I was raised as a boy, I was never capable of fathering a child or of penetrating a woman.

As a toddler, I was so tiny and frail that my parents feared losing me. At two years old, I weighed just eighteen pounds. At nine, I wore my six-year-old sister's dresses. I was the shortest of my classmates until fifth grade. Even in high school and college, I was one of the smallest of my peers. I liked being petite, but I kept growing into my early twenties.

My facial features are characteristic of Turner Syndrome. A small jaw makes my face more feminine than it would otherwise have been. Strangers complimented me on my pretty eyes, and people teased me for ears that stuck out. Because of my small size and pixie face, I thought that I might be a changeling. Perhaps an elfin half-girl was left in place of the human boy everyone seemed to expect.

I am so grateful that my parents encouraged imagination, curiosity, and a desire to learn. Even when that meant my reading books like *Heidi* and *Pollyanna*. Even when I asked for a tea set or a doll of my own. Or an Easy-Bake oven. Even when I asked my mother to teach me how to sew.

I have the spatial deficits common to Turner Syndrome—both visuo-motor and spatio-temporal. Dance and most sports are impossible for me to learn. Without hormones, I had very little muscle mass. I envied the boys their strength, speed, and agility, but I knew that I was not one of them.

In middle school, I fell in love with a boy. Not sexual attraction, mind you—I did not have the hormones for that, and I had no idea what people did to make babies. He sang Beatles love songs to me, and I dreamed of being his wife and the mother of his children.

> *Close your eyes and I'll kiss you.*
> *Tomorrow I'll miss you.*
> *Remember I'll always be true.*

"All My Loving," The Beatles

With my intersex body, I imagined myself a straight girl—or at least a straight half-girl. In high school, the boy I hung out with never knew of my dreams and aspirations. We were just a couple of teens spending a lot of time together, often with me on the back of his motorcycle, my arms tight around his waist.

For much of my childhood, I lived in my books—or ran barefoot through the woods—dreaming of what could be. I was not a real boy or a real girl. I knew that. But in any of the hundreds of science fiction and fantasy novels that I read, I could be whoever I liked to be.

I tried hard not to let my differences show. But that meant withdrawing from a cruel world. It was the consistent kindness of a Christian boy that led me to a childlike faith in Jesus. And it was my Savior who showed me that I had to participate in life in this world even though my hope was in the next.

Eventually, I became content with my body. Growing in spiritual maturity was an important part of coming to terms with the ways that I am different.

So will it be with the resurrection of the dead:
What is sown is perishable; it is raised imperishable.
It is sown in dishonor; it is raised in glory.
It is sown in weakness; it is raised in power.
It is sown a natural body; it is raised a spiritual body.

1 Corinthians 15:42–44
Berean Study Bible

Christians often tell me that intersex conditions are a result of Original Sin and the Fall. In other words, they argue that I should not exist at all—at least, not the way I am. They use my body as an example of how sin has corrupted the world.

Some insist that I must ignore my actual intersex body and view myself as male or female based on which sex I would have been had Adam never sinned. Some say that God's original purpose in creation is that anyone with a Y chromosome be male. Me. Male.

Sometimes, people want to declare me male or female because they get caught up in issues of marriage, sex, and procreation. But my body does not function like that, so why do they need to worry about how I might fit into a resurrected world? Is it important that I either menstruate or have erections for eternity? Do I—or does anyone else—need a functional reproductive system in heaven? What is the point? Why can I not be resurrected as intersex?

When the dead rise,
they will neither marry nor be given in marriage;
they will be like the angels in heaven.

Mark
12:25 NIV

I do not know how sex and gender will matter in the Resurrection, but scripture seems clear that sexuality and reproduction will no longer exist. So, what is the difference between my having an intersex reproductive system that does nothing and my having a functional male or female reproductive system that will never do anything? Will there be some new use for our male and female parts?

Mixed Gonadal Dysgenesis had a profound effect on me while I was growing up. Having a small and frail intersex body with a feminine face shaped my personality. I would have been a much different person otherwise. Jesus could, indeed, resurrect me as a male, with the face, body, and personality I would have had without Mixed Gonadal Dysgenesis. He could make me a real boy. Perhaps someone tall and strong, like my brother. God could even make that new person recognizably me to everyone else. But, it becomes difficult to imagine what would be left of *me*.

My face was shaped by Mixed Gonadal Dysgenesis. It is not the prettiest. But, it is feminine, it is mine, and I am content to have it. My life experiences as a person with an intersex variation are a part of what has made me who I am.

For you created my inmost being;
you knit me together in my mother's womb.
I praise you because I am fearfully and wonderfully made;
your works are wonderful,
I know that full well.

Psalm
139:13–14 NIV

Will all of the good things that have sprung from the brokenness of this world be destroyed in the Resurrection? Must I be raised to new life with a "perfected" masculine face, so different from my own? Is the male-female binary so precious—or so fragile—that all ambiguity must be erased? Did an intersex variation so thoroughly corrupt my body that, in the Resurrection, God must use the body that might have been mine had I been male? Can God not perfect an intersex body without making it something else entirely?

Or, has our obsession with binary gender become an idol? To those who insist that we will all be clearly male or female in the Resurrection, I ask this, "Why do you think so little of God?" All of nature eagerly awaits Christ's return. The Resurrection will be the culmination of the redemption of my being. Me. My soul. My body, too. I believe that my intersex body will be raised up in the last days, as an integral part of me. What was sown in dishonor will be raised in glory. Praise be to God!

I know that my kinsman-redeemer lives,
and that in the end he will stand on my grave.
And after I awake, though this body has been destroyed,
then from my flesh I will see God;
I myself will see him with my own eyes—I, and not another.
How my heart yearns within me!

Job 19:25
author's translation

Notes

Lianne Simon is a Christian housewife and the author of several young adult novels with intersex main characters (www.liannesimon.com). She is also one of the co-founders of Intersex and Faith (www.intersexandfaith.org), a nonprofit organization whose mission is to help communities of faith minister to those born with a body that is not entirely male or female. They hope to accomplish that via advocacy, education, and support.

"All My Loving" was released by the Beatles in 1963 on their album, *With the Beatles.*

Suggested scripture

Romans 8—Creation Groaning, Body and Spirit

Phillipians 1—Gratitude for Struggles That Show the Gospel

1 Corinthians 15—Paul's View on Resurrection

For further reflection

Have there been difficult, painful, or broken parts of your life that have also shaped you and made you who you are?

What parts of you do you hope will be changed or transformed in the Resurrection? What parts do you hope to keep?

Have you ever experienced God's love building you up in the face of confusing messages from the rest of the world?

Dear Pastor

By Rebecca Kerns

> *And let no eunuch complain,*
> *"I am only a dry tree."*
> *For this is what the Lord says:*
> *"To the eunuchs who keep my Sabbaths,*
> *who choose what pleases me*
> *and hold fast to my covenant—*
> *to them I will give within my temple and its walls*
> *a memorial and a name*
> *better than sons and daughters;*
> *I will give them an everlasting name*
> *that will endure forever."*

Isaiah 56: 3b–5 NIV

Dear Pastor,

I really do appreciate that you are trying to make me comfortable, but I have learned from many years of experience. Yours is not the kind of church community where I would want to open up about who God made me to be. More often than not, you do not really want *me*. Actually, I started backing toward the door as soon as your mouth shaped the words non-binary, gender dysphoric, transgender.

I understand that you want to seem compassionate. Yet, I know that within this twenty-minute sermon, you are going to *use* me (and the millions of people in this world who are like me).

You are going to tell the congregation that God knew us all, from the very beginning. And, you know, I am going to want that to be true. You are going to tell this congregation that, yes, God made man and woman, and then he made someone like me. You may even share that Jesus mentions us. You will use words like "atypical," "compassion," and "variation." In all likelihood, you will avoid the use of "disorder."

You have done your reading.

Here is the problem. Whatever your intentions may be, I am not here to be used by you. I am not here to be your object lesson. I steadfastly refuse to be your pawn.

167

You are correct that some of us are not clearly male or female—though some of us are and just have features that may surprise you. All of us lie somewhere on a spectrum that 80% of your congregation had never heard of before today. To you, we are the exception that proves the rule.

You will probably look at your big toe as you talk about us, without even understanding what we have gone through. Your voice will drip with pity—or maybe with a flourish that suggests that we are exotic. Of course, you will say that your congregation should walk with us in love and charity. Anyone who watches the live stream or video will know of your unimaginable love for us, the downtrodden intersex soul.

Your display of knowledge and compassion for us will make your words about our transgender, non-binary, and gender dysphoric siblings ring even more true. You, dear Pastor, are using us.

We see you. We all see you—and how you are using us.

We are not the abomination you get to point out, so that everyone will see your expertise and understanding. We do not want your compassion or your pity. If you want to walk with us, you need to recognize our strength and power.

While transgender people may seek surgical intervention so that their bodies can fit a little more clearly within the binary system you espouse, many intersex people wish more than anything that our bodies had just been left alone. Your compassion for us is extended because we do not fit neatly into your male and female binary system.

But, what you do not understand is that, by trying to make us fit, you have left too many of us surgically mangled, dependent on hormones, infertile, and forever at the mercy of physician after physician. Your praise for the binary system destroys the bodies of innocent children before they even learn the difference between a boy and a girl.

You want credit for working to help me find my place in your binary system, but that binary system tore apart my body before I was able to walk.

The first time I was met by discomfort like yours, I was divorcing my then-husband. He revealed the details of my physical anatomy to leaders of our church. He chose to discuss my chromosomes and hormones just to curry favor with the pastor.

This was the church I had attended since I was a teenager, and this was the pastor who had seen me through frizzy hair, braces, and even an ill-advised affection for plaid. As a family who adopted, we were praised in the church community. We were successful, interesting, boisterous, and fun, so our family was pushed toward the forefront of church happenings. Our faces were all over the videos played on the big screen in the front of the sanctuary.

We were really very visible. Until we weren't. Because of what they learned about my anatomy at birth, I was gently nudged toward the door.

Your words of compassion and condescension have no value for intersex people. I am here to charge you to fight for us. We are a part of the LGBTQIA world. We are the "I" that sits right there near the end of the alphabet soup. The "I" does not stand for "invisible." Please do not make us invisible.

If you want to show us compassion, love, and kindness, it is time to talk with us directly.

We want—no, we *need*—you to rail against all of the laws and precedents that are being written right now that will harm me and all of my LGBTQIA siblings. Speak out, saying that we are human, just like you and your children. Advocate for our right to marry, for our right to public accommodations, and for our right to work. Defend our right to compete in sports. Stand for our rights in every corner, from the bathroom at your local restaurant to the language being used in your social media feed.

People with intersex variations are equal. We are coming out of the shadows to show you the fullness of our humanity. We are here. We may or may not be queer. We might even be the nice Christian mom or dad sitting next to you on Sunday morning. We may be your grandchild or your best friend.

Do not *use* us. Full stop. Do not condescend, just to show your pity. I am not here to make you feel better about yourself.

Before you use us as a talking point, please stop to speak face-to-face with an intersex person. Ask us if your words are a dangerous knife or a welcome balm. If you do not know an intersex person, I can offer myself as a resource. I speak for myself, but I have access to an amazing community. We want to help you. Please be in touch.

However, know this. We are 1.7% of the population. So, you definitely know someone who is intersex. They just may not consider you someone safe enough to tell.

We are not your example. We are not your exception. We are not your dry tree. We, too, are the people of God. Our names have already been written on the walls of God's house.

So, dear pastor, thank you for thinking of us! But, I know you can do better.

Notes

Rebecca Kerns holds degrees in English and Religious Studies from the University of Missouri. She is a mom, a wife, a teacher, a student, and an unrepentant loudmouth. Sundays may find her in a pew or on a trail, holding church among the squirrels and deer in flyover country.

Suggested scripture

Isaiah 56—Eunuchs and Foreigners (see Chapter 13 of *OtherWise Christian*)

Matthew 19:12—Jesus and Eunuchs from Birth (see Chapter 14 of *OtherWise Christian*)

Jeremiah 1:4-5—The Call of Jeremiah

For further reflection

Have you ever experienced someone else's compassion in a way that made you feel "less than"? How did you respond?

Has anyone ever used you as an example of their familiarity with an entire category of people? How did you feel about it?

Do you feel well-educated about the diversity of experiences among people with intersex conditions?

A Revelation

By Mykal T. Shannon

God saw all that [God] had made,
and it was very good.

Genesis 1:31a NIV

As a member of the gender-expansive community, I am one of many who has been devastated by the ways that religion, specifically Christianity, has been used against us. While I eventually found my way, I can testify to the damage that has been done in the name of God.

I have grown into a Black transgender man who pastors a liberated and inclusive church in the Bible Belt of North Carolina: Dynamic Faith Ministries. Yet, to get to this place, I had to seek the Divine for myself (and often times *by* myself). I have landed in a place of peace about who I am and how my Creator views me, but there were times when being hit by one clobber passage after another felt earth-shattering to me.

While I was not born into the church, I was only seven when my father led our family into a Seventh-day Adventist faith community in my hometown of Cleveland, Ohio. I was exposed to a very strict religious practice with Saturdays spent stuck in church while all my friends were outside playing. At this early age, I was mostly learning Bible stories and how to "act right" in church. I believed whatever stories I was taught, from Adam and Eve in the Garden to Joseph's coat of many colors..

At that time, I was content to be a little boy (in a female body). I did not yet understand what kind of conflict this would eventually represent in my world. In my late teens, I began to understand that the way my body and spirit aligned might be problematic—but to the rest of the world, I was just a girl.

I had begun to have serious (secret) crushes on a few of my female friends. I knew enough to know that this would be a problem to both my family and to many others around me. I quickly learned the fine art of pretending. I only dated women in secret. If any relationship became long-term and we decided to live together, we would describe the arrangement as "roommates."

I perfected my pretending in the church. Any time a young man showed an interest, my mother and other women in the church would nod in my direction. This intensified the pressure to perform. I learned how to smile, just enough, to suggest there was possibility. I watched my straight friends carefully to learn the right gestures, but it felt less like a choice and more like an obligation. I had to be convincing, because I had to protect my secret at all costs.

While I had no words to describe what made me different, I still understood that both my parents and my church community would be upset if they knew about "it." If my church family was upset, then I assumed that God would be upset, too. One thing I knew for sure was that you did not want to upset God. I did not want a quick one-way ticket to hell!

Still, by my late twenties, I was starting to make poor decisions as I tried to cope with my double life. From the outside looking in, I had mastered this game, but the internalized deceit was getting the best of me. I resolved to move away and start over, minus the pretending. I still wanted to tell my mother the honest truth, whether she would accept me or not. I felt that I owed her that.

My father had passed away from cancer a few years prior. Mom was all I had left. I planned to have the conversation once I was settled into my new place in Charlotte, North Carolina. The day before I was to leave home and head south, my "roommate" called my mother and outed me. I was at work cleaning out my desk when I received the phone call. My mom was very upset, asking me if what she had been told was true. I had never felt so ashamed in all of my life.

I had worked hard to keep my family and friends in the dark. At some level, I felt that maybe this was some kind of evil spirit that might be *catchy*. Folk wanted to distance themselves from anyone or anything that was labeled "funny" (with a twist of one hand) or "queer" (when that was a *very* bad word). Maybe, I was contagious.

Yet, I was so desperate to be loved and accepted that I had stayed in an abusive relationship with an alcoholic. This was another reason that it was time to go—before my secret life unraveled through circumstances beyond my control. Nevertheless, now my secret was out.

My mother's unspoken worry had always been "what if the church found out." Mom wanted to be sure I knew that I did not get "this" from her. Somehow, I thought everything would be solved with a simple change of location. How wrong I was—and this was only the beginning!

Once in North Carolina, I learned *a lot* more about the issues between the church and the gay community. I was free of the "roommate" charade, but I entered into a time of deep exile. Mom sent me a constant stream of mail, denouncing my "choices" before the gods. She said she was worried about my "fall from grace," but her deeper shame showed through when she said, "don't tell the rest of the family about any of this."

Over time, Mom did come around. She became supportive and even seemed to enjoy a visit with me and my partner at the time. I was just glad to have my mom back. I would go through another separation from her when she realized I was transgender, but that is a story for another time.

It seemed as though life was settling down into a new but more authentic normal—except for my faith walk. I could not find a church that felt accepting and affirming. I underestimated how much it would hurt me to be told by church folk/leadership that I was broken, sick, and sinful. I was haunted by every scripture the saints had used against me. Once internalized, these voices of judgment became louder and louder. It was difficult to hear myself think. My own voice and experiences were being drowned out in the commotion. Eventually, I denounced the church entirely. I was tired of all the rejection.

Hey, if God didn't want me, I was not going to fight about it! I stopped looking for (or even hoping for) a church that would accept me. I put away all of my religious books and my Bibles. I packed everything about my faith walk in a box and put it as far back in my closet as I could—literally.

I had been rejected by a lover, by my original church family, and by many of my long-time friends. I lost control of how my Mom would learn about who I really was. God was just one more loss to add to the list. I was feeling exposed—butt naked, really—in this new place, but I was determined somehow to take a stand for my own integrity and freedom to be me. It was the only way I could figure to survive.

I spent the next 10 years in that exile running from my previous life of faith. Eventually, I stumbled onto an affirming church down the street from my apartment. I started to look more closely at many of the Bible verses that had been used to shame me. One by one, I discovered that much of what I had been taught was mistranslation. I got through each clobber passage with an affirmative result, except for one.

The creation story is the first story in the first book of the Bible, Genesis. Its familiarity is part of what makes it such a powerful weapon against us as gender-expansive people, whether non-binary, gender-variant, same-gender-loving, transgender, or even intersex. Time and time again, we have heard, "God made Adam and Eve, not Adam and Steve!" The simplicity of this assault went to the core of my (then) limited understanding of God. I carried around a secret sense of doom.

God started out with Adam and Eve "in the beginning." This seemed factual enough. As the argument goes, the absence of people like me from the creation story proves that we were never intended by God. If I could not see myself in the scriptures, then I imagined that the church folks might be right. Maybe, I *was* broken, sick, and sinful. Maybe, I needed to pray myself into straight-submission (which I had tried many, many times with no success). Maybe, I should go back to pretending.

I kept trying to reassure myself that God would work this out when I made it to heaven, but this intolerable logic haunted me, always in the back of my mind: What if they are right and I am wrong?

This went on for many years. No matter how much I studied the Bible, this old, childhood story tormented me. Believing that I was not included in God's plan also led me to destructive behaviors and eventually homelessness. Questioning my identity before God undermined everything for me.

Then, not long ago, God gave me a revelation that empowered me finally to stand, knowing that I am beautifully and wonderfully made just as I am (Psalm 139:14). I now understand that I am very present in the creation story of Adam and Eve!

Genesis chapters 1 and 2 tell two stories of the very first people that God created. They tell how the Author of Reality established the heavens and the earth. This sacred text tells us that everything that the Creator made was *good*. The heavens, the earth, the waters, the creatures of land and sea, the sun, the moon, the stars, and the separation of the waters—all good! Then, of course, as the story continues, we are presented with the creation of Adam (the first earth-creature) and Eve (mother of life). Still, all of it was *good*!

I finally realized that I, too, am good.

Our current reality was set in motion during those six days of creation. Yet, there are also many things that were created that were not mentioned in Genesis! Take sound, for instance. No one questions whether it is real or if it exists, but there is no mention of how sound was created either. If this was the case with sound, could it be the same for me?

The creation account does mention the creation of light. Yet, it was not until 1676 that Danish astronomer, Ole Roemer, discovered the speed of light (670,616,629 mph). While we are told that light was created, the story does not give us every detail about the light. God left plenty of details for us to discover on our own.

According to Genesis 1:14, the moon was created to give light to the night and to provide for the seasons. In 1686, Issac Newton helped us to understand that the moon is also responsible for the tides in the ocean. Newton studied the Bible daily, but he did not let the creation story distract him from observing the world around him. It is also God's *good* creation that the moon moves the waters. However, there was no mention of this purpose in the beginning, in Genesis.

An eclipse occurs when the moon passes between the earth and the sun. This spectacular phenomenon was not documented until 1375 BCE by the Babylonians. However, that does not mean it was new. An eclipse happens in any one area once every 360 to 410 years. It is uncommon and atypical, but that does not mean it is broken, sick, or sinful. The potential for this phenomenon was established when God put the celestial bodies into motion at the start, even if humankind remained oblivious for quite some time afterwards. Yet, eventually, we caught up with God's purposes.

I praise God for the beauty of a sunrise or a sunset, even though the scripture says the day and night were to be separated. We do not shun beaches, swamps, and marshes, just because they blur the God-given line between the "dry land" and the "gathered waters," as told to us in scripture.

Should we allow social norms to ridicule that which is unusual, like the eclipse? Should we condemn the moon because it is more influential than the scriptures describe? Should we ignore every sound except the very voice of God, because we have no record of its creation?

No. There are many behaviors *established* in the original creation that were not mentioned in the biblical text—from scientific details to the beauties of the natural world. These, too, were God's *good* creation, even though they are absent from the poetry of Genesis 1–2.

Inside of each tree is the potential for paper, chairs, tables, and many other useful tools. This possibility was also a part of the original creation at the beginning of time, even though it did not become visible until later on when humanity seized upon that potential. The promise of such wooden tools was not mentioned in the creation account, but it remains very real and a very fruitful part of our lives today.

In the modern world and global economy, it may seem that we are discovering a great many new things for the very first time. However, it is arrogant for us to imagine that such new encounters did not also emerge from the Mind of God. Later developments are not less valuable, less credible, or less entitled to exist.

I finally realized that the dark clouds of my life had arisen, not from my lack of faith, but from the biased assumptions that I had been fed since early childhood. Some would say that people like me were not documented in those very first stories. Even if that is true, that does not make us any less valuable or real. I was *born* into the fabric of the human race, *just as I am*, in the story of creation, waiting to be discovered.

This revelation—that all things created were not mentioned in the Genesis account, even if not discovered until later—gave me life again! This was a resurrection of the faith life that I had before I was confronted with social norms and gender biases. I had conquered the last of many Bible references that stole my peace. This text had caused me to doubt myself, to feel unworthy, and, yes, to believe that I might be sinful and outside of the will of God. That was a lot to carry! I am so glad Spirit has given me this

resolve. God is good and created me to be *very good* indeed!
So, I celebrate all of God's creation story:

Adam and Eve

Adam and Steve

Sheila and Susan

The Mx community

The Bi Nation

Trans Folx

Poly Folx

Pansexuals

Metrosexuals

Asexuals

and all the gender-variant individuals not listed here, including
those that have yet to be *discovered*.

We were *all* there in the beginning—in the Mind of God, as a part of the
Divine Plan, waiting to be revealed. Praise be to the Creator of all things!

Notes

The Rev Mykal T. Shannon is the founding Pastor of Dynamic
Faith Ministries, Inc., based in Asheboro, North Carolina, while also serving
the Charlotte, North Carolina, community. He is passionate about lending
support to his trans community and providing a safe worship space for all
people. His first book, *Trans Expressions: The Many Faces of My FTM Journey*
was published in 2019. Watch www.mykaltshannon.com for additional
offerings. Pastor Shannon is also hosting an OtherWise Adventist
discussion group on Facebook (and perhaps beyond). Visit
www.otherwisechristian.com for more information on how to join in.

Suggested scripture

Genesis 1–2—Creation Stories

Psalm 139—God Knows Us Intimately

Romans 8:31–39—Nothing Can Separate Us

For further reflection

Have you ever wrestled with gaps in the biblical testimony?

How has God continued to reveal Godself to you through creation?

What comforts you and helps you to be more authentic in relationship with God?

Balance

By KimiFloyd

Now the serpent was more crafty
than any of the wild animals
the Lord God had made.

Genesis 3:1a NIV

I am *Aaná'kimaa'tsis* (ah-knee-ah-key-moo-ah-ta-seeee-it-seea). In the Siksika (Blackfoot) tradition it means "lantern light." I am *Skíinaattsi* (ski-knee-ah-taa-see), which is both "dark" and "night." I am light and dark, night and day, two halves of a single whole, two-spirit. The Siksika language does not declare gender in the same way that English does. For example, *oostówaaway ni aaná'kimaa'tsis* translates as "s/he is the lantern light." In English, the default is two specific, gendered pronouns ("he" or "she"), but the Blackfoot language defaults to a general pronoun, the equivalent of "they" (singular). The Siksika believe that the sun is a specific being. So, I am lantern light.

I am also *anaukitapi* or Métis, which are both terms indicating that I am mixed-race. My great grandmother was *Niitsitapiiksi*, commonly known as Blackfoot. This word means "the real people." Our traditions teach us to be honest and good beings, caring for each other and our created world. My ancestors were Blackfoot, Mahican, Delaware, Muskogee, and African as well as Irish, Scottish, English, and Swiss.

My name, reclaimed from my ancestors and given to me, is "Kimi" which means secret, and "Floyd" after my father and grandfather. Kimi is pronounced "kee-mee" with the i's sounding like the "i" in "police" or "elite." However, my mother called me Kimberly, and since most people knew me as Kim, I have defaulted to allowing that pronunciation for my name most of the time. Still, in my heart, I hear the correct pronunciation echo, delivering hope and strength from the ancestors.

I am not Kim, or even Kimi, I am Kimi Floyd—the two names reflecting the two halves of my whole. I am often reminded that this is an experience many transgender people share—this reclaiming of the names that are etched in our hearts, even if they were left off our birth certificates.

179

Blackfoot spirituality is not a religion. Instead, it is a way of being in the world. We find strength in our ancestors, remembering how we should be and want to be through the lessons of those who came before us. Our stories and traditions connect us to the earth and to the celestial sky, as well as to each other—to those who walk beside us and those who have gone ahead.

There is wisdom in both the light and the dark. Naato'siwa (Nah-too-see), the sun, was the first being created by the creator God Apistotoke (ah-piss-toh-toh-kee). Unlike the personified Christian God, Apistotoke is a divine spirit without human attributes. Apistotoke is also sometimes known as *Iihtsipaitapiiyo'pa* (ee-tsih-pie-tah-pee-yoh-puh) which means "source of life."

Naato'siwa means "holy one" and embodies the hunter and warrior spirit of the Siksika. He is often called Na'pi (sounds like knobby) which means "Old Man." Kipitaakii (kih-pih-tah-kee) or "Old Lady" is the moon-spirit and lifegiver, nurturing and caring for the heart of the people. While Na'pi and Kipitaakii are seen as light and dark, male and female, that does not imply that one is more than the other. In our tradition, this pairing only points to the way that that there are always two halves of any whole. In fact, some of our legends say that Naato'siwa was the child of Kipitaakii, making Kipitaakii the mother and nurturer of the first creation.

To be two-spirit is to bring two halves back together, to heal division in myself, and then help end the oppression of my people. When I stand and affirm myself as two-spirit, I am rejecting centuries of language and violence that tried to deny my existence, my humanity. Being two-spirit is more than gender or sexuality. It means walking the earth while remaining in touch with the spirit world. People often appropriate the term, using it in a generic way without understanding what they are really claiming. Two-spirit means always striving to do greater good in the world.

I replenish my identity through ritual and sacrifice, visiting the Medicine Lodge to renew my connections to the ancestors, and practicing meditation between those visits to maintain those connections. Two-spirit is not another name for queer. To be two-spirit is to be a part of indigenous culture and religion. My Siksika faith teaches that, without darkness, there can be no light. Joy, freedom, and authenticity must all be renewed and replenished. In nature, summer is the time of growing, but if winter does not happen the soil cannot be ready for the seeds to take root. Like the earth, we are replenished through a cycle of light and darkness.

In the stories of those who have sought and found freedom from oppression, whether that is from forces acting on their body or forces reacting within their body, we learn our own path. When I share my past, it is a lesson that we can survive even when our path leads through valleys and challenges. In the fifteenth year of my life, my light was almost extinguished. I had found the strength to tell my mother and stepfather who I was, that I embodied both male and female, and that I was attracted to people, not genders. Colonization meant disconnection from those ancestors who could have helped me walk this path with honor.

After I revealed my truth, I was sent to a place that tried to make me reject one half of myself for the other. A supposedly religious man told me that if I refused to push my truth back down, I would burn for all eternity. He used images and words to inflict pain. He used fear to condemn me for being who I am—and I believed the lies he told because he masked them in the language of love. I spoke my truth again and again but found only more rejection. Finally, I tried to stop that pain for good, but I survived and reclaimed myself from the ashes of those lies.

Ancient people, including the Canaanites and Phoenicians in the biblical text, believed in the Phoenix, a bird with brilliant plumage of red and blue. After building its own funeral pyre, with a flap of its massive wings the bird immolates itself, cleaning all that needs cleaning in an instant of resurrection and hope. Many cultures had a similar mythological being— the Egyptians had the Bennu, some Native Americans believed in the Thunderbird, the Japanese had the Hō-ō, and others used other names, but each represented the hope found in transformation. I sometimes wonder if those myths also reflect transgender and two-spirit people within those cultures, affirming the beauty they brought to the people. The ancient people knew that there is always a risk in the process of rebirth. Some Phoenix do not survive, and we must remember even those that are lost in the midst of change.

The Creator God—called by many names—sees the beloved-ness of transgender people. That is why we were gifted to the world. I am both male and female. I am neither gay nor straight. I am neither white nor Indian. Instead, my deepest strength is found in my very identity as a person who cannot be defined by the binary categories of humanity.

Both the Siksika and Christians tell stories of snakes. In Genesis, it is a serpent that leads the first man and first woman to the Tree of Knowledge. In biblical lore, the serpent is evil and stays evil. But, in the Siksika tradition, Snake is redeemed through love. The story of the snake who would become a warrior has been told over many campfires and many centuries.

An evil Snake wandered the world striking out at Siksika people, killing them instantly. But, one day, Snake met a maiden, the child of a chief, and fell in love with their kindness. As the maiden passed, the snake resisted all they had been told they *should* be (as an evil snake). The snake could not bite this beautiful foot.

Knowing that there was no hope for any maiden to love a snake in return, Snake fell very ill. They were taken to a wizened medicine person, who, after hearing the story, prayed to Apistotoke for transformation. The medicine person called many other wise people to help. Soon, the voices of many prayers joined together to help guide Snake down the path of transformation. After many days, the chanting stopped. A young warrior stepped from the tent where the snake once laid by the fire. The love Snake had for the maiden had transformed Snake into a leader who cared for the people. The chief welcomed Snake and they spent the remainder of their alive-time serving the people who had given them new life.

To fully understand the snake's story, one must understand the archetypes of the warrior and the maiden to the Siksika. Maiden and warrior were not specifically limited to one gender but reflected a person's heart. The warrior societies of the Great Plains tribes include the stories of many great female warriors, including Pitamakin (Running Eagle), who led the Blackfoot people after soldiers murdered their spouse. Pitamakin was born Otaki (or Brown Weasel Woman). They were a maiden and became a warrior.

Pitamakin is honored today in Glacier National Park in Montana with a lake and a waterfall—each bearing Pitamakin's name. The waterfall was selected because, in the spring, water pours over the upper falls, hiding the beauty that lies beneath. In summer and fall, the upper falls dries up and then water begins to flow from a hole that remained hidden in the rock wall. The white men called it "trick falls," but it is officially known as Pitamakin Falls, because it embodies transformation. Pitamakin died in 1832 and is the only woman-born warrior who was given a male name by the Blackfoot people.

I am often confronted with the common understanding of the Christian story as one of rejection. The snake is condemned to slither the earth. The first woman is condemned to suffer pain in childbirth. The first man is also ejected from his home. The rejection of that instant of judgment follows their descendants through generation after generation, as they try to find their way back home.

If this is the beginning of the Christian faith, what does this say about the traditional Christian faith? Is rejection the most important part of the story, or have we gotten it wrong by focusing on a single moment instead of a longer journey? Wouldn't the story be deepened if we refocused on the great gift that transformation can be, no matter how it begins? Adam's and Eve's departure from the garden was hard, but it would also lead to Bethlehem and the birth of Jesus who is the center of our faith.

In contrast, the Siksika story is *always* read as one of redemption and affirmation. Snake knew they were meant for more than simply striking out at people who got too close. The people of the tribe forgave and welcomed and affirmed all of Snake's possibility—all of who Snake wanted to become. The Siksika affirm and embrace the power of transformation, even when it involves Snake.

The Siksika story is one of hope and love, but the Christian story is not dissimilar if we look at it with a new and refreshed lens. We get so caught up in what was lost before that we ignore the power of the transformation that comes after. Adam's and Eve's story is remembered for that moment under the tree, but they also had children and grandchildren. They lived for many years after they left the garden. They lived full and productive lives after their transformation. When we ignore that part of the journey, we reduce their story to a single moment of trauma, erasing the decades of healing love and life that followed.

Some have rejected me for being two-spirit—for accepting the deepest transformation of my body, mind, and spirit; but, as Snake found, God answers and guides us through quests of transformation—onto the path that will bring us to our own journey toward wholeness.

Notes

KimiFloyd is a narrative storyteller and writer, drawing on healing stories from many cultures and places to guide people to a deeper understanding of who they are and who they want to become. They earned their Master of Divinity degree at United Theological Seminary of the Twin Cities in Minnesota and are currently working on a Doctoral degree in Public Theology with research into the lives of two-spirit, transgender, and other queer people of faith, especially in rural areas. KimiFloyd serves as the Program Minister for the Open and Affirming Coalition of the United Church of Christ.

KimiFloyd uses "two-spirit" (with a hyphen) reflecting Algonquin teaching and usage which treat it as one word, just as it represents one person with two halves, undivided. The Siksika language is a hyphenated language when translated—meaning that many Siksika words and phrases need multiple words or phrases to communicate the same thing in English. Broader pan-Native usage may vary.

Suggested scripture

Genesis 3—Adam, Eve, and the Snake

Ecclesiastes 3:1–8—A Time for Everything

Matthew 5:14–16—You Are the Light of the World

For further reflection

What stories remind you of or affirm your identity? Do any of your names hold meaning for you?

Have you ever tried to force strong feelings or an authentic part of yourself into hiding?

How has your journey brought transformation and change to your character?

Phoenix Bones

By Caedmon D. Grace

> *In Greek mythology, a phoenix is*
> *a long-lived bird that cyclically regenerates*
> *or is otherwise born again.*

Wikipedia

> *The hand of the Lord was on me,*
> *And he brought me out*
> *by the Spirit of the Lord*
> *and set me in the middle of a valley;*
> *it was full of bones.*
> *He led me back and forth among them,*
> *and I saw a great many bones on the floor of the valley,*
> *bones that were very dry.*

> *He asked me, "Son of man, can these bones live?"*

Ezekiel 37:1–3 NIV

And then, I was taken by the Spirit of the Lord to a valley of dry bones.

She, Sophia, Wisdom from God, spoke to me without words. She played my memories like the Ghost of Christmas Past, showing my own life to me as if I were an observer. I was able to see and *feel* the history of these dry bones.

It was not the people of Israel who had perished; it was all of the adventurers, the seekers, the dreamers and the prophets—the visionaries, the rebels, the seers and the guides, the healers and the lovers. These were the bones of my people.

Day by day with micro-aggression after micro-aggression, victimization after victimization, neglect after neglect, disappointment after disappointment, lie after lie, fear after fear, we have lost our ability to trust

185

our own Truth. A deadly stronghold steps in, slowly silencing our voices: the injury of broken eye contact because so many people cannot bear intimacy; the unknown rules, the unmarked boundaries, the tides of change; and the rugs being pulled out from underneath us.

Among these bones, I could see the *ruach*—the life force, the breath of the universe—becoming shallow in their bodies, as if it were my own memory. The pressure pushed them into theory, into rhetoric, toward surrender, and toward suffocating under the weight of the world.

We know when we are not believed in. The world has taught us that we will not be seen. Unknown by others, we simply stop showing up. We begin to silence ourselves before anyone else can reject us again. We give up the very *knowing* that makes us who we are. We begin to forget ourselves.

All of this came to me in a moment. I could *see* my own despair—my own dry bones. I asked Her, Sophia, "How did I survive?"

Silence.

I pleaded with Her, "Why am I here?"

The silence continues.

My impatience and agitation grew.

Eventually, venom spilled out as all of this history, my own history, landed deep within me: "Stop fucking abiding with me. I do not want to see these things. I do not want to feel these things."

More silence.

Somehow, I knew what she wanted from me. I knew I was about to break through a painful emotional wall—a wall that was there for a reason. This was going to hurt.

"I cannot do what you ask of me," I spat at Her, spewing more frustration. "Here I am. Yet, now, you want to *stop* speaking to me, Spirit?! Say something!"

Silence.

More silence.

So much more silence.

In the face of Her unresponsiveness, I stopped speaking. Yet, my own wordlessness betrayed a silent rage. I was eager for an adversary in this argument. In contrast, *Her* silence emanated peace and even acceptance. I could feel Her Love.

Her continuing presence evoked even more anger in me.

I knew that I was in a metaphor—a dream or a vision. I could not get out. I felt trapped. I felt overwhelmed by what was happening—by the way she was pulling me into Her presence and Her vantage point. I wanted to be back in my own body, back in a more familiar kind of control. I wanted to be back in the reality to which I was accustomed—insulated once again from all of this Truth. I wanted to escape the sheer awe of that moment. It was terrifying.

I believe that a moment should be able to stand alone. No history. No future. To be fully present in a given moment is to leave behind past and future. Yet, *this* moment was something different. This moment required a different kind of presence—something deeper and all-encompassing. She was inviting not just *me* but my past and my future, too. She wanted all that I am, all that I have been, all that I will be to *abide with* Her, immersed in this pure sense of potential and possibility.

Finally, she asked, "Can these bones live?"

I was fed up with riddles and ambiguity—fed up with parables and paradox. This was beyond personal. She meant, "Can *your* dry bones live?"

"Quit messing with me," I said while trying to squirm away. "There is already enough grief and loss and death. There is no need to dwell there."

Silence.

She began to play my memories back to me.

SCENE 1

She showed me how he was a manipulator, an exploiter, and a liar. "It's not that safety isn't possible, Beloved, but that you were not safe there," She said.

I stopped dead in my tracks when She spoke.

"What did you just say?" I asked.

She repeated Herself, "It is not that safety isn't possible, Love, but that you were not safe there."

She showed me another memory.

SCENE 2

She showed me how it was the pain in my mother's body that made her distant when I needed her. It was her guilt and fear that made her angry. Sophia spoke again, "It's not that you're unlovable, Love, but you did not get the love you deserved."

I yelled back, "Excuse me? You can't talk to me like this!"

Yet, it was also a painfully, sweet sensation—that of the Divine Love of God bearing witness to my pain and speaking answers to the questions I had long since stopped asking.

"It is not that you are unlovable, Dear One, but that you did not get the love you deserved."

I was dumbfounded. How could all my angst dissolve after just a few words of validation from my True Love. Were my puzzles solved? Would my questions cease to exist?

SCENE 3

She reminded me again, replaying a series of sexual encounters from my past. By now, I was curious about what else She might say to me. One by one, she corrected the meanings I had made out of these various encounters.

"It is not that you are too affectionate, Love, but that she hated *her* body."

"It is not that you are incapable of understanding her feelings, Love, but that *she* was unable to say what *she* meant."

"It is not that your body is broken, Love, but that those people were not able to see you for who you are—and *that* was *not* love."

These declarations from the Spirit of Life, from the mouth of God, carried such force that the air began to swirl around me.

My awareness shifted, and I began to notice that the sun-bleached, white bones had disintegrated into red and orange ash. Like dust rising to fill the sky, the ash arose and began to take shape.

She spoke again, "So tell me, Wise Warrior, can these bones live?"

I was so taken by the glory I felt around me—the fullness that comes from being seen by my Divine True Love—that my heart soared. I felt whole again.

How could there be any doubt that these bones can live?

By just one Word from God, I have found the Source of light within. Now, there can be no more excuses, no more stories, no more attachments.

She asks, "Can the dreamers dream again?"

I can tell by the way she posed the question that the answer is yes! Now, I was beginning to feel ready.

"Can the healers heal again?" Yes.

"Can the seers see again?" Yes.

A bird-like head formed from the ash—with a long sharp beak and a stance that was big and powerful and strong. It grew with long extended wings that were on fire and trailing long, ornate, tail feathers. I was watching in awe at the majesty of color and form, seeing the process of life coming from death, hope from despair.

She continued, "Can the prophets find their voice?"

I knew that the answer was, "Yes."

"Wise Warrior, what say you? Can lovers learn to love again? Can soulmates find their way home? Is there any child of humankind who might be found trustworthy? Will you choose to believe? Wise Warrior, do you believe?"

I was absolutely stunned. My heart awakened.

How is it that all this power to believe *still* lives in me? Why does the quality of my life hinge on what I believe about existence? How, in the face of all those dry bones, can I hope? I realized that my entire life hinged on how I was perceiving the world. If I perceived a threat, I would feel threatened. If I perceived possibility, I would feel hopeful. Everything turned on a dime, depending on *my* vantage point.

I *can* choose to believe in a world that I can see with my heart but not with my eyes. I can dwell with Her, with the Divine, in Possibility, even in the midst of these dry bones.

My heart decides before my mind does.

I, too, turn to deep red and orange ash—my beak; my head with the regal feather brow; my body sprouts wings of fiery feathers. I could taste the delicious irony that even this becoming was a part of my own dying—which would become the very substance and form of my next incarnation.

"Soar over the ash, Wise Warrior, and see how it feels to give Life."

I did not know what She meant, but I flapped my wings and flew up above the ash that had been stirred by the wind. As I was soaring about, all at once the remains of the dreamers, the lovers, the seers, the healers, the prophets began to rise. The ash became an entire flock of Phoenix birds, hot and bright as the sun.

I flew back to the Spirit's side. I was quiet now.

In my heart, I felt that I should apologize for my doubt and disheartened demeanor, but, before I could speak, she said, "Look!"

She steered my gaze toward the valley. There were no bones left— not even the ash. In fact, there was no sign whatsoever of what had just happened, except at the very edge of the horizon. I could just make out the fleeting visage of a red-orange Phoenix tail as it flew free.

I was completely awestruck.

Then, I heard Her say, "Why the silence…?"

I took a deep breath and I began to speak.

Then you, my people, will know that I am the Lord,
when I open your graves and bring you up from them.
I will put my Spirit in you and you will live,
and I will settle you in your own land.
Then you will know that I the Lord have spoken,
and I have done it, declares the Lord.

Ezekiel 37:13–14 NIV

Notes

The Reverend Caedmon Grace is an educator and spiritual healer who serves as a board member of Transfaith. He is an empathic, intuitive Christian clergy with the Metropolitan Community Church (MCC) of San Diego, California. MCC is a historically queer movement within Christendom.

Pastor Grace takes his name from the 7th-century poet and mystic. According to the English historian Bede, Caedmon was a simple man who tended to the animals of a monastery. The legend says that Caedmon knew no poetry of the type commonly shared as oral tradition at the time (often celebrating battles). He avoided singing because he was embarrassed that he was not more literate, but, one night, he was given a vision in his sleep that would change the course of his life. Caedmon would go on to become a monk who offered songs of beauty and praise for God and creation. "Caedmon's Hymn" is the earliest surviving poetry of its kind. The legend suggests that Cedmon's hymns and poetry were based on dreams, such as that first, fateful visitation. Translated from the Old English, Caedmon means "wise warrior."

Suggested scripture

Ezekial 37—The Valley of Dry Bones

Psalm 33:6—*Ruach* (Spirit, Breath, Word) from the beginning

Proverbs 8:22–31—*Sophia* (Wisdom) from the beginning

For further reflection

Have you ever had a dream or a vision that brought you new clarity or hope?

What images of resurrection and new life resonate most strongly with you?

What resources have helped you to recover from trauma and abuse?

Afterword

Claiming Our Stories

By Mx Chris Paige

Stories are powerful—from the biblical testimony to our own. Yet, the world too often tells OtherWise-gendered people that our stories are unimportant, if not invalid, shameful, or inappropriate. Indeed, antagonistic Christians are quite accomplished at launching stories of their own that characterize us as deceitful, predatory, sick, or sinful. There seems to be something frightening about our truth. As Erin Swenson wrote in her reflection, there is a kind of "existential rage [from our] accusers."

I once heard Elena Rose Vera preach a sermon at the Transgender Religious Leaders Summit in Berkeley, California and she would later allow us to reprint it in Transfaith's *Being Brave Together* handbook. She eloquently makes the point that transgender people are inspiring and controversial because of our integrity. She argued that it is neither some kind of shapeshifting magic, nor long-suffering sacrifice that sets us apart. We are no more perfect or saintly, broken or depraved than any other demographic. However, our choice to pursue the truth, no matter what the cost may be, is a defining characteristic.

> I believe in trans people. I believe in us because we have been honest, at least once, in a way few people on earth have been asked to be. I believe that is what makes us so frightening. That integrity is written all over us. ...
>
> Integrity is contagious, see. It is hard to look at the way we know the truth and not be tempted to look at your own truth, and that truth's consequences. It is hard to pretend, with us in the room. It is hard to make excuses for your own lies and compromises and little self-betrayals. So, people try very hard to make us the liars. To make us the fakes. To push us out of the room so we don't hold mirrors up.
>
> It's not that we're special. It's just that, every one of us, whatever we did before or since, we made a choice. We believed. We committed. We moved. With everything mobilized to erase us and keep us from truth-

191

telling, we had the strength of spirit to choose truth anyway. (excerpted from "Holding On" by Elena Rose Vera)

Certainly, a similar argument could be made about people with intersex variations. Doctors (and some parents) push people with intersex variations into the shadows, inviting them to be ashamed of their God-given bodies. Yet, increasingly, intersex activists are breaking through their isolation to find one another and to tell their stories. This, too, is powerful resistance in a world that profits from misinformation and half-truths. This, too, is a model for how all of us might be more truthful and courageous in our own lives. Whether we are resisting religious antagonism, social marginalization, medical malpractice, or cultural expectations, claiming our deepest truths is always sacred work.

As we were approaching the finish line for *OtherWise Christian 2: Stories of Resistance*, I brainstormed with our authors about the #TransphobiaIsASin campaign. This campaign was started by J Mase III and Lady Dane Figueroa Edidi as a way to disrupt and heal from religious and spiritual-based violence and harm. The campaign is intentionally bold in terms of naming transphobia as "sin"—using that concept, so often weaponized against OtherWise-gendered people, to claim our liberation.

However, as I corresponded with our authors, some had reservations about deploying a term with as much baggage as "sin" carries. Meanwhile, our authors with intersex variations struggled with how they might work with the transgender-specific nature of the campaign. In the end, we came up with a friendly alternative that seemed to work for everyone—and our #SacredOtherWise campaign was born.

So, we want to invite you to join us in claiming our stories by claiming your story, too! You can testify to your truth by sharing images and stories on social media using #TransAndSacred, #IntersexAndSacred, #NonBinaryAndSacred, or #TwoSpiritAndSacred. However, our goal is not to pressure anyone into disclosing truths that may put you at risk. Rather, we want to bless you with our collective testimony that truth-telling, story-sharing, testimony-making is sacred work. Whether you use these hashtags (or your own variation) or not, we encourage you to claim the power of your own story—whether you share that story in public, with friends/family, or simply in your own private journaling.

If nothing else, the Bible shows us that stories of struggle, resistance, and resilience are sacred and enduring, as they are passed down from generation to generation. So, whoever you are and wherever you are on your journey, I hope that you have been touched by something that has been shared in these pages. I hope that just maybe we have been able to pass along some nugget of hope or wisdom through our "stories of resistance." Perhaps, as you close this book, you even will have gained some new understanding of and appreciation for what might be possible when OtherWise-gendered people of different shapes and sizes are embraced and celebrated.

So, in the words of Jesus, I invite you to go into the world and share that testimony, as well. "Truly, truly, I tell you, we speak of what we know, and we testify to what we have seen..." (John 3:11a Berean Study Bible). May you receive our testimonies with compassion and grace. May you go and tell others what you have seen and what you have heard. May you celebrate and support the stories of resistance that may show up when "folk like us" appear in your own life.

Thanks be to God. Amen.

Appendix A

What is "OtherWise-gendered" and the OtherWise Christian series?

By Mx Chris Paige

OtherWise Christian 2: Stories of Resistance is an anthology of reflections, which are separate enough that they could each stand alone. However, this project also builds in many ways on my first book, *OtherWise Christian: A Guidebook for Transgender Liberation* (2019). In particular, the idea of "OtherWise-gendered" people honors a wide variety of identities and experiences that have been suppressed or marginalized in the Western world. In chapter 2 of the first book, I explained it this way:

> *OtherWise Christian* [1] invites us to read the Christian Bible and the development of Christian traditions with some historical context, while grappling with the ways colonization continues to shape our thinking about sex, gender, race, and religion. Efforts toward transgender liberation will necessarily have limited impact when they fail to embrace in full measure these traditions of resilience and resistance. This means that we must question again and again the ways that our language and pre-existing ideas may shape the way we perceive both the world and the text.
>
> I will use "OtherWise-gendered" to mean "any gender identity or expression that transcends the simplistic Western settler-colonist narrative of two and only two mutually exclusive and unchangeable genders, defined strictly and easily based on biology at birth." "OtherWise-gendered people" includes both modern "transgender" people as defined by Merriam Webster as well as some (not all!) modern intersex people. However, the definition here has to do with resisting or transcending Western settler-colonist gender ideology, rather than suggesting that transgender and intersex experience are the same. Meanwhile, "OtherWise-gendered" also stretches to embrace gender identities and expressions that are based in other cultures, worldviews, and understandings (for example, two spirit, *fa'afafine, waria, muxe, hijra,* etc).
>
> When I say "OtherWise-gendered," I am pointing to the wisdom and insight of a gender-full resistance. I am pointing to the many kinds of people whose life experiences have been trampled on or confined by

Western, settler-colonist assumptions and ideology. As such, it is important to be clear that OtherWise-gendered is not a singular experience or way of being. Rather, OtherWise-gendered is an effort to open the doors and the windows to make more space for us to listen earnestly to the diversity of God's good creation in all its many gender-full forms. (*OtherWise Christian*, page 8–9)

OtherWise Christian 2 is just one step in bringing such gender-full life experiences to the fore. God willing, the OtherWise Christian series will continue with several more volumes.

If you think that you might have personal reflections like those found in *OtherWise Christian 2: Stories of Resistance*, please be in touch! Additional OtherWise Christian volumes are anticipated, and you are invited to contribute!

> One volume will focus on reading the Bible and Christian tradition specifically from the perspectives of **people with intersex variations**.

> Another will look at OtherWise-gendered experience in light of **Catholic and Orthodox traditions**.

> Another will explore the process of moving from Christian perspectives dominated by fear toward the frequent, "**Be not afraid**" admonitions of scripture.

You do not need to be a trained theologian or a professional writer. The world needs our testimonies! Please be in touch if you think you might have a "story of resistance" that you might want to share—that is, a story about how your OtherWise-gendered life has been shaped by Christian tradition. Contact me at **otherwisechristian@gmail.com** and let's discuss.

Next Up: *OtherWise Christian 3: What Shall Prevent Me?*

Chapter 15 of *OtherWise Christian* [1] looked briefly at the Ethiopian eunuchs in Acts 8 and Jeremiah 38. Meanwhile, Mir Plemmons gave us an intersex reading in *OtherWise Christian 2*. Yet, there is so much more to be explored in this powerful story of the first Christian baptism—the baptism of an OtherWise-gendered person of African descent who would become the first Christian pastor and evangelist. *OtherWise Christian 3* will provide space for us to explore the many dynamics around **this Acts 8 traveler** in more detail and from more points of view.

I am currently collecting personal and biblical reflections about the significance of this story for OtherWise-gendered people. Reflections from the African diaspora are especially encouraged, along with reflections from OtherWise-gendered people of all sorts as well as the allies who travel with us. Contact me at **otherwisechristian@gmail.com** to get involved!.

Appendix B

How many people with intersex variations are there?

Compiled by Mx Chris Paige

There is no consensus on how many people with intersex variations exist. In her reflection ("Gender Diversity and Christian Community") in *OtherWise Christian 2*, Virginia Mollenkott used the numbers from her research in 2001:

> As many as four percent of all children are born with degrees of both male and female genitalia, and one person in five hundred has a chromosomal composition other than XX or XY. (Mollenkott)

Privately, Donovan Ackley III ("Every Body is Good. You're Welcome.") provided some more recent figures:

> Depending on definition of "intersex," 1 in 60 to 1 in 10,000 people are born with an intersex condition (from *Fixing Sex: Intersex, Medical Authority, and Lived Experience* (2008) by Katrina Karkazis, page 23).

In her reflection, Rebecca Kerns ("Dear Pastor") states, "We are 1.7% of the population," reflecting a number that is commonly used by intersex activists (similar to the 1 in 60 figure used above).

The truth is that we just do not know. "Like everything else related to intersexuality, the reporting of frequency rates is a matter of heated controversy" (Teri Merrick, 2013, from an unpublished manuscript, provided by Donovan Ackley III). In conversation about how we should handle such statistics in this book, Mir Plemmons ("The Ethiopian Eunuch—and Me") commented:

> First, you have to decide what your definition of intersex is. If you are only including chromosomal composition that is a low number. If you go to the other side and include all the secondary sex-linked characteristics

that make people indeterminate or less able to experience life as cisgender or endosex, that is a much different number. Frankly, there is very little real data about us. (Plemmons)

Nick Manchester ("Doctrine") breaks it down further:

One of the big issues with determining "intersex numbers" is that data is really not tracked on us. For instance, if you check with academia and media (*Scientific American*, for example), there are only a handful of "recognized" chimera. I and all of my chimera friends laughed long and loud, because none of us were among the five that are officially "recognized."

Unfortunately, this is how the "hide intersex and make it rare" game is played. The safe number recognized by intersex rights organizations is 1.7%. The real number is likely much higher, but that also depends on a person's definition of intersex. This gets into a whole conversation about gatekeeping, which is also problematic. Of course, no gatekeeping is also problematic as we have seen many trans people somehow wanting to prove themselves to be "intersex."

1.7% is safe and is out there in wide publication, especially on the international level, but I would be glad for us to lean into the data that says there are more of us—because there are. (Manchester)

In the end, it should not matter "how many" there are. Lianne Simon ("Resurrected Bodies") spoke for all when she clarified:

I do not think there is a consensus on which conditions are intersex and what the numbers are. People tend to argue for lower numbers if they are conservative and higher numbers if they are progressive. I like to entirely avoid the numbers because, even if there are only a few hundred of us, we are still created in God's image and have the same basic human rights. (Simon)

Amen.

With much gratitude to our intersex authors!

Acknowledgments

I would love to honor the significance of each and every author, but I will save that for the blog. However, I want do to single out Vicky Kolakowski here for offering such a potent historical perspective in the Foreword. The Reverend Honorable Kolakowski is better known for her historic break throughs as an openly transgender attorney and judge, but I like to call her the Queen Mother of Transgender Theology. It is not even 25 years since that first article. We have come a long way, but we are also quick to forget how we got here. I am proud and grateful that Vicky's voice is included here.

In addition to the authors, this work would not have been possible without the community that we call Transfaith. While OtherWise Christian books are not projects of Transfaith, there are many board members, staff members, volunteers, funders, donors, supporters, and other collaborators who helped make this work possible simply because they made Transfaith possible. With the possible exception of Virginia Mollenkott and Erin Swenson, who were visible and known to me before Transfaith was born, every author in this book is someone I have come to know through the work that we have collectively done together.

It would be impossible to name everyone who contributed to or supported Transfaith, but Louis Mitchell, my Transfaith co-founder, deserves specific mention. I would not be who I am today were it not for Louis's willingness to share this journey with me through so many toils and troubles. Furthermore, Louis has been shaping our work together for a couple of decades in a variety of ways.

The phrase "holy hybrid" belongs entirely to Louis, and I am delighted that his chapter in this anthology makes that plain. While I always want to affirm the benefit of a deep dive into a particular tradition, transgender folk are courageous boundary-busters who often experience a time of wandering in response to rampant trans-antagonism in Christian culture. As a result, the lines between different faith traditions among transgender folk often break down in practice. We are "holy hybrids," and a variety of offerings in this anthology demonstrate that dynamic.

The other community that I want to mention is *The Other Side* magazine, where I worked for nearly a decade. It was my day job when I started that little website called *Transfaith Online*, so in that sense, *The Other Side* has supported this work from the beginning. But, more specifically, three of the articles in the first section of this anthology were first printed in *The Other Side* at about the same time Virginia Mollenkott's *Omnigender* was going to press in 2001. The influence of that work was far-reaching, even if not well documented. Articles from *The Other Side* would go on to be cited in Pat Conover's *Transgender Good News* (2002), Justin Tanis's *Transgendered* (2003), and elsewhere.

Working with transgender authors was almost unheard of in 2001. Unfortunately, it remains a relatively rare commitment in Christian publishing to this day. Still, it is a testimony to the quality of that work that a cluster of articles from almost 20 years ago remains relevant today (with minor updating). Back when Transfaith was just a quirky hobby of mine, *The Other Side*'s editorial staff did something no one had ever done before—at a time when there was really no pressure to do so. So, I want to honor that important editorial work, as well as the community of staff, board, authors, donors, subscribers, and readers who made such prophetic publishing possible for as long as it lasted.

Meanwhile, as the publisher of *The Other Side* at that time, I also acknowledge that representation of people of color, transgender men, and people with intersex variations was absent in that first attempt. I am proud that this anthology expands significantly on that first foray, even though it still fails to provide a complete picture. I am already planning additional volumes to address some of the remaining gaps.

I am grateful that Nancy Krody, once again, offered expert copy editing advice for this book project. As one of the co-founders of the United Church of Christ Gay Caucus in 1972, she knows first hand what it is like to be on the cutting edge of emerging Christian movements. Now retired from her long-time work at the *Journal of Ecumenical Studies*, Nancy remains a persistent ally and supporter of both Transfaith and OtherWise Engaged Publishing.

I am grateful to my daughter Nevaeh for putting up with endless conference calls, book events, and piles of books around the house. You give me hope.

Last but not least, I would be nothing without my parents, Ron and Carolyn Paige—literally, of course. However, I also think that listening is probably the most important skill for building an anthology of diverse voices like this. When I think back, I know that I learned to listen from your example.

May the rest of the world hear our voices, too.

Mx Chris Paige

OtherWise Reflection Guides

from OtherWise Engaged Publishing

Christian Faith and Gender Identity: An OtherWise Reflection Guide (2019) by Mx Chris Paige is an entry-level resource, which provides a gentle introduction to transgender experience in the context of Christian tradition. This booklet includes scripture, modern definitions, reflection questions, and more.

In Remembrance of Me, Bearing Witness to Transgender Tragedy: An OtherWise Reflection Guide (2020) is a series of short meditations that unpack deep wisdom around themes such as grief, self-care, repentance, and our ancestral traditions. The booklet includes reflection questions and additional resources, including liturgical resources.

Paperback books are available from the publisher at a discount if you order multiple copies.

Sign up for updates from OtherWise Engaged Publishing to hear about other new releases as they become available!

Please visit http://otherwiseengaged4u.wordpress.com to learn more.

The OtherWise Christian series

from OtherWise Engaged Publishing

OtherWise Christian: A Guidebook for Transgender Liberation (2019) by Mx Chris Paige is a resource that looks at 25 years of transgender-affirming biblical scholarship and includes an extensive bibliography of additional resources. There is also a free *OtherWise Christian* group discussion guide. Mx. Chris Paige argues that the Bible shows us story after story of OtherWise-gendered people being used by God to further the kingdom. Yet, we have been bamboozled by a restrictive gender ideology that is aligned with empire, white supremacy, and Christian supremacy. Jesus and our biblical ancestors invite us to join a gender-full resistance!

In *OtherWise Christian 2: Stories of Resistance*, Mx Chris Paige has gathered together 29 transgender, non-binary, two spirit, and intersex authors to share about their lived experience in relationship with Christian tradition. Having provided a detailed survey of relevant scripture in *OtherWise Christian*, Mx Chris now brings us a survey of testimonies from actual OtherWise Christians in this new book. Reminding us that the discussion of gender issues is not a theoretical one, this collection provides insights into the ways that Christian tradition has served as both an obstacle and a resource for OtherWise-gendered people in the modern world.

Paperback books are available from the publisher at a discount if you order multiple copies.

Sign up for updates from OtherWise Engaged Publishing to hear about other new releases as they become available!

Please visit http://otherwiseengaged4u.wordpress.com to learn more.

About the Editor/Author

Mx Chris Paige

Mx Chris Paige is the author of *OtherWise Christian: A Guidebook for Transgender Liberation*, publisher of OtherWise Engaged Publishing, and blogs daily at otherwisechristian.com. Mx Chris was founding executive director of Transfaith and publisher of *The Other Side* magazine. They are available for speaking, teaching, and preaching engagements.

Praise for *OtherWise Christian*

"In this invigorating dive into scripture ... Paige reads the Bible in provocative ways to affirm support for transgender experience. ... surprising yet plausible. ... strong and imaginative. This is a treasure chest of resources for those interested in ways transgender individuals can live faithful to God and to one's self."

Publishers Weekly

"This is the book that we need."

The Rev. Terri Stewart
United Methodist Alliance for Transgender Inclusion (UMATI)

"The most exhaustive look at gender non-conforming/trans identities in the Bible that I have seen to date. Informative & accessible."

Peterson Toscano
Transfigurations: Transgressing Gender in the Bible

"I am excited to revisit familiar characters and narratives with a new OtherWise lens. This is an extraordinary gift to the trans community and to those, whether transgender or cisgender, who wish to go deeper in the texts to see those of us who have been hidden, erased, and/or disparaged."

The Rev. Louis Mitchell
Executive Director of Transfaith

"... a truly incredible book. Mx Chris' writing is clear, elegant, and prophetic, and the book's intertextual readings of scripture and popular culture are very insightful. This book beautifully answers the deepest possible question: how can we imagine and practice our spirituality in ways that are truly just and liberatory, especially as it concerns our gender."

Cleis Abeni/Upāsikā tree
Transgender elder

"... a wonderful resource... This is a faith text that CANNOT be ignored."

The Rev. Shanea D. Leonard
Associate for Gender & Racial Justice for the Presbyterian Church (U.S.A.)

"... a brilliant yet down-to-earth, supremely compassionate and practical guide for how religious people who don't fit binary categories can engage with and draw strength from the Bible... "

Dr. Joy Ladin
The Soul of the Stranger: Reading God and Torah from a Transgender Perspective

OtherWise Engaged Publishing

OtherWise Engaged Publishing is excited to be working with the best and brightest of OtherWise-gendered folk! We provide a multi-tradition, independent publishing operation for projects from OtherWise-gendered folk that are in alignment with our values.

Visit otherwiseengaged4u.wordpress.com
for information about our latest releases
and to support independent transgender-led publishing.

What are the words you do not yet have?
What do you need to say?
What are the tyrannies you swallow day by day
and attempt to make your own,
until you will sicken and die of them, still in silence.

~ Audre Lorde

CPSIA information can be obtained
at www.ICGtesting.com
Printed in the USA
FSHW020857150320
68049FS